"Linderman's book is bo
implores us to reconside
to regain that childlike w............ how we fit in the world. For
Linderman, this is not just some clever thought experiment; it is
a matter of our survival. He contends that we must sift through
the wheat and chaff of what the Enlightenment has taught us,
placing our 'spirit' subjective selves back at the center of a new
kind of thinking, in order to propel us forward. It is a deftly
guided and joyful journey that challenges how we think and
encourages us to wonder about a better way."

—**Michael Metzler**, Enrichment Instructor,
Rochester Institute of Technology

"Mr. Linderman has the highly focused purpose of reaching out
to those of us who are overly infected by Enlightenment thinking—and who isn't?—and providing the foundation for a mode
of thinking that should engage everyone who reads about it and
will astonish everyone who truly understands it."

—**Frederick Dennehy**, honored New Jersey attorney

"Linderman demonstrates how consciousness evolves...helping
me understand the development work we do at Sekem."

—**Ibrahim Abouleish**, Founder of Sekem, winner of the
2003 Right Livelihood Award

"Linderman's aim throughout is to illustrate for the reader new
to this material how what he calls 'The Belief'—belief in the
largely unstated assumptions that have grown up around the
practice of the physical sciences—prevents nearly all of us from
seeing the reality outside of it, whether over, under or beyond."

—**Terry Hipolito**, Independent Scholar

"Linderman's excellent book helps us understand exactly why
so many of our textbooks are bound and locked up in 'The
Belief'.... So many of us have a sense that the textbooks need to
be rewritten, but are not quite sure with what. Linderman helps
us answer this most important question."

—**Bill Manning**, honored Minneapolis attorney

WHY THE WORLD AROUND YOU ISN'T AS IT APPEARS

a study of Owen Barfield

ALBERT LINDERMAN PhD

Lindisfarne Books | 2012

2012

LINDISFARNE BOOKS

An imprint of SteinerBooks / Anthroposophic Press, Inc.
610 Main St., Great Barrington, MA 01230
www.steinerbooks.org

Cover and book design: William Jens Jensen

LIBRARY OF CONGRESS CATALOGING-IN-PUBLICATION DATA

Data available on request

ISBN 978-1-58420-121-2 (paperback)
ISBN 978-1-58420-122-9 (eBook)

CONTENTS

ACKNOWLEDGEMENTS

I owe thanks to a number of friends and colleagues without whose help this book would not have been written. Two friends who had a hand in the book long before I ever conceived of the project, Barbara Verble and John Shirk, met me for coffee and talked with me about the topics that fired our passions for knowledge. Perhaps most important in moving me along the road to an understanding of Owen Barfield's thought was Greg Marsh, a friend of my business associate, Jeff Baker, who introduced us. On a handful of occasions Greg allowed me to grill him while he patiently explained his understanding of Barfield's thought. Our discussions were enthralling and he remains a friend and discussion partner. In addition to Greg, Bill Manning, whom I met in the most serendipitous way I've ever met anyone, and who owns a complete set of the works of Owen Barfield (at the time, more than half of Barfield's writings were out of print), and who willingly gave time for discussion and continues to teach me much.

When I first began contemplating writing this volume, Kate Clark helped guide the organization of the writing and encouraged me when I was unsure of the value of the work. Others such as Peggy Jewett, Sheryl Grassie, Joe Voelbel, and Liz Moertel offered help on specific sections. Several more also helped or encouraged at various points, including Steve Chicoine, Anne Moertel, Terry Hipolito, Jane Hipolito, Robert Slocumb, Herbert Klem, Charles Kraft, Gertrude Hughes, Frederick Dennehy, Michael Metzler, Emma Bate, Emily Ann Roy, Hilary Lund, Emilie Hitch, and Ed Emerson. Gene Gollogly has been a friend that has provided much encouragement along the way. Particular thanks go to the two who helped edit the manuscript—Lee Linderman, my son, who led the editing/clarifying process, and Laura Linderman, my daughter, who assisted in editing the work and also provides an excellent sounding board for bouncing ideas back and forth.

INTRODUCTION

"Imagination is more important than knowledge. For knowledge is limited, whereas imagination embraces the entire world, stimulating progress, giving birth to evolution."
—ALBERT EINSTEIN[1]

Human evolution is often talked about as a physical transformation occurring over millions of years. But another type of evolution has also been taking place over the span of human existence on the planet. This evolution impacts us much more directly. It involves the way we perceive and think, and its pace is accelerating as we navigate the early part of the twenty-first century. Though primarily a phenomenon of Western civilization, this evolution influences our entire world because of the tremendous political, social, and economic power wielded by the West. However, most of us do not see this evolution, nor understand it. It has not become part of the mainstream of thought of Western society. Until it does, our world will experience more complex and more dangerous problems.

We must begin to see in a broadened, more improved way than we are used to seeing ourselves and our world. In the argument presented in this book, I make the case for this new way of seeing that I call the New Enlightenment. We need it to supersede the Western world's current theory of knowledge (i.e., way of seeing). Incorporating this wider view to knowledge will allow us to build societies that can face the challenges brought about by longer lifespans, depleted natural resources, and a growing world population. Fundamentally, this book is a book of hope for our individual and collective futures.

Consider:

---

1   Viereck, "What life means to Einstein: An Interview" (*The Saturday Evening Post*, Oct. 26, 1929)

In the small villages of the Gutu district of Masvingo province in Zimbabwe, there are many centenarians despite the droughts that have devastated neighboring regions. Their means of survival holds keys that may assist African leaders in feeding the massive numbers affected by the cyclical droughts that plague the continent.

Centuries-old methods of agriculture involving the precise "reading" of the positions of the stars and planets—a "reading" which is said to make potent certain minerals that are applied—are being used across Egypt in the cotton industry as the methods have proven to be superior to modern, Western means of growing cotton.

In many health clinics across the United States, more and more naturalistic, Ayurvedic, Chinese, and mind–body methods are being incorporated into the practices of family practice clinics and alternative hospitals.

At a leadership program for Daimler, at a regional health care summit in Frankfurt, Germany, and at an MIT think tank, leaders practice a meditative method that allows them to foster access to the source of new ideas and the morality connected to the ideas.

In Chichen Itza, a Mayan ruin in the Yucatan state of modern Mexico, the interplay between the sunlight and the edges of the steps on the pyramid create a shadow display on the northern stairway during which a jagged line of seven interlocking triangles appears to be a long tail leading downward to the carved stone head of the serpent Kukulkan, which resides at the base of the stairway. The snake's body appears only briefly, and only on the equinoxes—and has done so for a thousand years.

These seemingly random vignettes have much in common. They come out of a way of thinking and perceiving that is little known in the West and rarely taught in our schools or championed in our public policy. The way of thinking that has evolved in the West no longer allows us to see how the examples above work. To understand how they work requires a different consciousness—that is, a different type of thinking.

"Just Give Me the User Interface"

Recently, I surveyed a number of people and asked, "How do you come to know anything, and have confidence in what you know?" Some responded by referring to a religious or spiritual source for knowledge. Some expressed ignorance as to how to answer the question. Most expressed adherence to rational thought and the evidence generated by scientific investigations. None discussed how their mind and thinking processes work. In one sense this is not surprising. It is much like most computer users who want a smooth running user interface without knowing how the software is designed and configured.

How we think is something we take for granted. Most of us know quite a bit more about how Windows or iPhones operate than we do about our own thought processes. We live life unaware of the inner workings of our own minds. Whether you realize it or not, you engage the world around you according to a theory of knowledge that you learned growing up. That theory of knowledge is inadequate for today's world.

Part of the reason we do not pay attention to how we think is because we have not been taught its value. Unsurprisingly, then, no one I interviewed mentioned their mind or their thinking processes as the bases of their knowledge. Ask yourself: When is the last time you thought about how your five senses convert sensory data into meaning? When have you concerned yourself with how meaning is interpreted from one language into another? For most of us, likely not recently.

If you have been raised in North America or Europe, or have been educated in the manner common to the traditions of Western civilization, you are my audience. The Enlightenment of the eighteenth century brought about a way of thinking that dominates Western civilization today. As citizens of Western societies, our minds all work somewhat alike. We have inherited, through our parents, education system, language, and mass media, the patterns of our predecessors' thought. This inheritance goes deep into our subconscious. Our failure to recognize this may limit our future in a potentially dangerous way. I call this way of thinking—the legacy

of the Enlightenment that most of us in the West take for granted—
"The Belief."[2]

Hardened by popular science, embedded in public discourse, and emphasized throughout our lives by most authorities, "The Belief" firmly concludes that our five senses give us the truth, the whole truth, and nothing but the truth. Furthermore, "The Belief" argues that this truth is the *only* basis for understanding a reality that is believed to consist primarily of solid objects. Policies, grants, and political and social leadership are generated and governed by this fact-verifying belief system. Syndicated columnists and spokespersons from the nation's largest newspapers, web sites, and broadcast news programs write as if it goes without saying that "The Belief" is true. But is it? How can we know that our five senses truly are capturing the "reality" around us?

As this book unfolds, I use examples, such as the ones in the vignettes above, to illustrate the inadequacy of the current way of thinking common to all Western societies. Understanding the way that New Enlightenment ideas are changing "The Belief" will allow you to begin to understand how to use new ways of thinking in your own life. You may never again look at yourself, your family, your neighbor, or the world in the same way.

Evolution in Human Thinking

So, how does thinking happen? What causes us to think the way we do? What difference does it make how we think?

A look at human history shows an evolution in the way humans think. From the nature-connected tribes of preliterate earth, through ancient Greek mythology, to our modern technologically sophisticated societies, human history demonstrates that long periods of relatively unchanged ways of thinking are followed by times of significant change characterized by increased novelty and innovation. Much that is happening in our world today indicates this is one of those times of change.

---

2   I use the terms *Enlightenment thinking* and *The Belief* interchangeably
    throughout this book.

Thinking Always Implies Consciousness

When we look at how humans think now and compare it with how humans previously thought, we are, by definition, bringing consciousness into the discussion. We can only truly think about what we are conscious of. Not only has the way humans think evolved and changed, our consciousness has changed as well. This has more implications than those that appear at first glance.

It would be hard to overstate the value of understanding what is happening currently— why it is happening and how these kinds of changes work. The quotation from Einstein above, with its reference to the "imagination," indicates the direction Western society must journey. Within a relatively short period of time, perhaps as soon as in the next fifty years, most of our children will be educated to think in ways that are quite different than those we currently employ.

Let me take you on a journey to introduce you to the deepest parts of your mind, to the very nature of thought, imagination, and potential. As we journey we will use new lenses to look at some of the world leaders in this new way of thinking, including American family physicians, MIT professors, and cotton growers in Egypt. As you take this journey you will be challenged to reconsider many long-held beliefs and perhaps begin to solve the following paradox of American life.

The Paradox

No one is more popular, more "mainstream," than Oprah Winfrey. Her cable network (OWN) and O magazine constantly introduce us to alternative thinkers. Guests such as endocrinologist Deepak Chopra, *Time* magazine contributor Andrew Weil, and former head researcher at the National Institute of Health, Candace Pert, draw insight from sources as diverse as ancient Hindu Scriptures, medicinal practices of the Hopi Tribe, and the mind–body practices of Tibetan monks. Paradoxically, despite Oprah's immense popularity and integration into many peoples' lives, our society does not view many of these guests as mainstream. If we did, we would allow these "alternative," "new age," and spiritually focused thinkers a more central role in the development of our public policy, educational programs, and health care. Many of these accomplished individuals are ignored or opposed by entrenched religious, political, educational, and scientific power structures. Though popular, they continue to be labeled "alternative" in the press and in the opinions of the majority of Americans. Are Oprah's popular guests, many of whom claim dependable sources for knowledge not gained through standard scientific thought, simply deceived? Or are there sources of knowledge that can be accessed without going through modern scientific channels? If so, how can we know these alternative sources of knowledge are logical and rational and not just the whimsy of charlatans?

I am convinced that this paradox results from our failure to understand how we think. For most Westerners, the logic of "The Belief" effectively closes the door to any other way of thinking. Mainstream vs. alternative, allopathic (Western medicine) vs. naturopathic, quantitative vs. qualitative, science vs. religion: Why the duality, why the disconnect, why the paradox? To unravel the paradox, we must move our thinking beyond its current belief that scientific fact is the only means to understanding our world. In order to do this, we must understand how our current ways of knowing came to be and how we come to know the meaning of anything. This will allow us to evaluate the framework for New Enlightenment thinking. This framework will help validate the experience of many who are currently viewed as alternative, while also showing how this new way of thinking can move mainstream scientific understanding well beyond its current limitations.[3]

---

3   My intention is to write in a way that will be accessible and understandable for the average reader while establishing the foundation upon which more expansive ideas beyond those offered by science can be brought into our world and experienced as truth. This will allow us to begin to address more effectively the major issues of our time because we will understand them more fully. I hope the book will help you identify causes, initiatives, and projects that spring from this new way of thinking and that need and deserve support. In addition, as you read, you may also begin to develop and strengthen your own way of thinking. I expect some of you will become re-enchanted with the world and the incredible capability of the human mind. I wish to engender that touch of wonder—a sense of familiarity along with a sense of

"The Belief," Imagination, and Einstein

"The Belief" as a theory of knowledge became a dominant way of thinking soon after the Enlightenment in the eighteenth century. It trusts only knowledge that arises from sense experience and can be verified experimentally. We see this crystallized by scientists and philosophers such as Francis Bacon and John Locke. Basically, these philosophers advocate distrusting or rejecting knowledge that may arise intuitively or from the interplay of ideas in the mind. In a famous citation found in dozens of books and articles throughout the past 400 years, Locke stated, "All knowledge is founded on and ultimately derives itself from sense, or something analogous to it, which may be called sensation."[4]

Ironically, however, the Enlightenment also birthed the remarkable quality of complete openness. This aspect of the "scientific spirit" sparked the imagination of many great scientific thinkers such as Einstein, Isaac Newton, and Charles Darwin. Einstein took issue with Locke and the spirit of "The Belief." In the quotation at the beginning of this introduction, "knowledge is limited, whereas imagination embraces the entire world, stimulating progress, giving birth to evolution," he points out that intellectual advances in the world come through the use of the imagination, not through mere sense-based knowledge. Many are startled by that assertion and assume that Einstein means something other than what the statement appears to mean literally. One of the basic reasons the statement startles is that our education system does not consistently and consciously teach about, encourage, or practice the use of imagination, particularly in the higher grades. Additionally, we do not have a usable agreed-upon theory of the imagination. As a result, typical graduates of public schools do not have the mental framework to discuss or use their most valuable latent ability.

---

strangeness—something you thought you knew or at least knew in part and now realize how much more there is to know. I hope this will lead you initially to understanding, eventually to awe and deep appreciation, and ultimately to action that will benefit our world.

4   Cranstron, *John Locke, A Biography,* p. 264.

One result of this is that the value of alternative thinking has been systematically marginalized across modern society. Despite the fact that psychology studies have shown that music fosters enhanced learning and imagination,[5] or that software engineers create best by not having to follow deadlines, the Western framework continuously rejects the inherent added value of novelty connected to performance. In my own field of cultural anthropology, one cannot even receive a grant without outlining a quantifiable argument. Moreover, the Federal Drug Administration, which oversees medical research, has rules that significantly limit and constrict the opportunity for innovation through alternative means. These facts point to the idea that, on the whole, society has reached a sort of reasoning impasse.

The Western world in general does not realize that most of the major advances in science have come through imaginative thinking. Many of Einstein's stupendous accomplishments, which are responsible in large measure for moving physics beyond its classic Newtonian moorings, grew from his original thought experiments. These include both his theory of general relativity and his work with gravity and light.[6] Only later did experimentation confirm his imaginative ideas. Copernicus, Galileo, and Isaac Newton all used imaginative thinking that did not follow the "common sense" of the day. It took years (in the case of Copernicus, 300 years) for their imaginative ideas to be demonstrated via experimentation.[7] In many respects, these scientists were all alternative thinkers of their times. Yet, society generally does not give credence to "alternative" thinkers. This relates directly to the fact that we do not have a theory that allows for knowledge to be drawn from sources other than those of empirical science.

Language and education have nurtured in Westerners a worship of the classic science of "The Belief." The New Enlightenment theory of knowledge results in a comprehensive alternative

---

5   Many studies are readily available, one of note, E. Schellenberg, "Music lessons enhance IQ" (*Psychological-Science:* Aug. 2004, vol. 15(8):511–514)

6   Beautifully detailed in Isaacson, *Einstein: His Life and Universe.*

7   Two works that chronicle these stories are Kuhn, *The Structure of Scientific Revolutions*, and Bortoft, *The Wholeness of Nature.*

to "The Belief." The alternative is not a reversal or elimination of "The Belief," but rather a theory that addresses the Enlightenment, shows its limits, and surpasses it.

Why this Book?

In essence, empirical knowledge is only one side of "reality." Empirical knowledge is all about the "outside," the surfaces of objects, the matter we can see and touch. It does not speak to the "insides," the unconscious inner reality, subjectivity, feelings, and meaning that humans contribute to the world of objects we experience in our day-to-day lives. The New Enlightenment looks at the inside from that place phenomenologist Edmund Husserl termed "the great world of the interiority of consciousness."[8]

Moving from Alternative to Mainstream. This book is also intended for those who appreciate the insights of alternative thinkers but feel at the mercy of an engineer neighbor, an amateur "science buff" friend, or skeptical relatives. They confidently present clear, reasoned, scientific arguments to discredit or, at least, bring considerable doubt to the veracity of the claims of the alternative thinkers you find compelling. For you to explain why you find some alternative writers so helpful, you need to be able to articulate succinctly the theory of knowledge that undergirds them. Likely, you struggle to do so now. You should find help in this book.

The New Enlightenment will provide a basis for "alternative" thinkers to be viewed as mainstream. You don't have to go far back in history to see a large change parallel to the one I suggest. At the beginning of the twentieth century, psychology had not gained widespread acceptance as a discipline. It was received with widespread skepticism. With the work of Sigmund Freud and Carl Jung, this skepticism began to change. Acceptance of this discipline began to increase dramatically. Throughout the twentieth century, psychology moved from a non-mainstream discipline to one now considered mainstream. Themes you will find current in psychological literature, such as emotional intelligence, optimism, and adult

---

8   Husserl, *Introduction to Logic and Theory of Knowledge.*

maturation, are recognized as both valid and utilitarian by most segments of society. As an example of just how mainstream psychology has become, many employment aptitude tests use insights gained from psychology to assist in hiring practices. The Myers-Briggs Inventory, the Minnesota Multi-phasic Personality Inventory (MMPI), and similar tests are common tools drawn from psychology and adapted for the mainstream workplace.

Mind and Matter. One core sticking point in articulating a new theory of knowledge concerns the issue of "mind." Whether the term used is *soul, Mind,* the Greek *Logos, vital force,* or *Self,* almost all alternative thinkers assume a realm of existence that is "made of" or consists of something non-material. They have not been successful, however, in explaining this in a way that is clear and powerful enough to engender a critical mass of society to believe that their way of seeing the world is valuable and enriching. Their explanations are either too difficult for most to understand (e.g., Ken Wilber), not sufficiently comprehensive enough to handle skeptics and critics (e. g., Deepak Chopra), or, as in the case of some Buddhist writers and practitioners, rooted in a mindset that does not fit into our Western way of thinking.

Another difficulty in creating a new theory of knowledge is the lack of cohesion in the approaches taken by many of these writers and their followers. They believe in their idea, but they have not been successful in tying it in with other alternative ideas. It's as if they have a puzzle piece but not the picture that shows how the piece fits. At the same time, understand that I am not critical of the insight many of these writers and thinkers have. Wilber and Chopra are two I enjoy reading and learning from. Many others have much to bring to our society. We lack, however, a common vocabulary and basic premises that can become common parlance for the New Enlightenment. I hope this volume will help rectify that.

For readers new to this topic, learning about all of this is much like the first time an older adult uses a computer and learns to use a software program. The array of icons, symbols, and key combinations seems overwhelming to understand, and only through a concerted effort of use and practice can all of these options be

Introduction

learned. It always helps to have someone who knows the program. That's one of the roles I hope to serve in introducing you to this theory of knowledge.

New ways of thinking can be learned. You may be wondering if your way of thinking can be changed. Recent neuroscience research into brain plasticity shows that not only can one's way of thinking change, but doing so will have direct effects on the material of our brain: The brain's physiology will literally change simply by thinking in a certain way for an extended length of time.[9]

The phenomenon can be illustrated by imagining your brain as a field of tall grass that separates point A, the origin of any given thought, with point B, the rationalization of the thought. In order to get from point A to point B, your thoughts travel along the same paths over and over until they are worn-down and well-traveled. If you are a post-Enlightenment Westerner, "The Belief" way of thinking only allows certain types of paths to be formed. Trying to forge a new path through the untouched tall grass inevitably results in reverting back to the "easy" path that already exists. However, concentrated efforts of thinking differently over time might allow one to slowly mat down the tall grass and, in effect, remake the brain's pathways. It is not an easy journey, but it may open up new conduits to alternative thought.

Introducing Philosopher Owen Barfield

I owe much of this book's major themes to Owen Barfield, an English philosopher who lived and wrote during the twentieth century (1898–1997). He expounded upon both the limitations of Enlightenment thinking and the new type of thinking described in this book. His particular focus concerned the nature of language and its influence on how we think. One of his major premises was the idea that language evolves reality as it changes over time.

Barfield wrote a dozen books and more than a hundred published articles and essays. He may be most widely known as a

---

9 Studies are too numerous to mention. A good start for research on neuroplasticity is the popular article by S. Begley, "How Thinking Can Change the Brain" (*Wall Street Journal*, Jan. 20, 2007)

WHY THE WORLD AROUND YOU ISN'T AS IT APPEARS

member of "The Inklings," an Oxford University group of thinkers that included C. S. Lewis, J. R. R. Tolkien, and Charles Williams. He was a major influence on the thought and writings of Lewis and Tolkien and drew the admiration of T. S. Eliot, W. H. Auden, US Poet Laureate Howard Nemerov, and Nobel Laureate Saul Bellow.

As Bellow stated, "We are well supplied with interesting writers, but Owen Barfield is not content to be merely interesting. His ambition is to set us free...from the prison we have made for ourselves, by our ways of knowing, our limited and false habits of thought, our 'common sense.'"[10]

Barfield's Connection to C. S. Lewis

Barfield's connection to C. S. Lewis warrants further mention. Lewis, in his autobiographical book, *Surprised By Joy*, described Barfield's philosophical prowess: "When you set out to correct his heresies, you find that he forsooth has decided to correct yours! And then you go at it, hammer and tongs, far into the night, night after night...you modify one another's thought; out of this perpetual dogfight a community of mind and a deep affection emerge. But I think he changed me a good deal more than I him."

Lewis wrote "he towers above us all" and dedicated his first scholarly book, *The Allegory of Love* (1936), to this "*wisest and best of my unofficial teachers*," stating in its preface that he asked no more than to disseminate Barfield's literary theory and practice. Regarding Barfield's unique intelligence, J. R. R. Tolkien wrote,

> [Barfield] was the only man who could tackle C. S. Lewis making him define everything and interrupting his most dogmatic pronouncements with subtle *distinguos* [distinctions]. The result was a most amusing and highly contentious evening, on which (had an outsider eavesdropped) he would have thought it a meeting of fell enemies hurling deadly insults before drawing their guns.[11]

---

10 As quoted on the cover of Barfield, *Saving the Appearances*.

11 Giddens, *J. R. R. Tolkien, This Far Land*.

Barfield has gained a significant following in both the academic and philosophical communities, particularly in the United States, where he was often a lecturer and visiting professor at several colleges and universities, including Brandeis and UCLA. Barfield's work concerning language and meaning is viewed with a near reverence by poets ranging from T. S. Eliot to G. B. Tennyson to American Poet Laureate Howard Nemerov.[12]

Reading Barfield's Writings

Why not just read Barfield directly, you ask. Reading Barfield can be difficult, particularly if you are not generally a reader of philosophy. I hope that after you read this book, you will pick up his writings. Having read this book, you will be prepared to understand his theory and can more easily follow the trail of his thoughts.

Beginning Our Journey

For many of you, the journey you will undertake while reading this book will challenge the core of who you are and how you believe life works. You will focus your attention on thoughts and ideas unlike any you have considered before. It will be as if a flashlight illuminates some of the deepest parts within you. The journey may be uncomfortable at times, perplexing at others, and often illuminating and exhilarating. In brief, this book argues the following:

1. Human consciousness[13] and language evolve simultaneously
2. The Enlightenment and its corollary (scientific thinking) marked one of the major changes in the evolution of human consciousness and, consequently, in the way humans think and perceive the world around them
3. In order to think scientifically, previous ways of thinking *had* to be effectively eliminated—and they were
4. Due to scientific thinking, Western societies have entered into an unprecedented era of material wealth. This

---

12   Note the foreword and cover quotations on Barfield, *Poetic Diction*.

13   I am defining *consciousness* as "awareness," whether awareness of a thing or a process (i.e., a particular experience or the mere passage of time).

same thinking, however, has led to a correspondingly unprecedented number of mental health, environmental, social, and individual problems

5. To address the problems facing our world, a new way of thinking is indeed emerging

6. To open our perception to this new way of thinking, we must understand the physical and mental processes involved in thinking

7. The power of our imagination will allow us to evolve to this new way of thinking and will open a means for us to develop an expanded science

To argue these points successfully, I will draw upon examples from areas in which New Enlightenment thinkers are already active and making an impact on our world. These include naturopathic medicine, mind–body connections, biodynamic and organic farming, and the building of ecologically sensitive communities. These examples will illustrate how New Enlightenment thinkers are challenging "The Belief" and building upon it to lead us into a new way of thinking that will quite literally change the way we see the world.

I hope that by studying the examples presented in this book, you will begin to understand how and why you think the way you do and how "The Belief" has put a stranglehold on any other way of knowing. You will learn how you receive and interpret sensory input through the senses of hearing, seeing, feeling, touching, and tasting. You will also begin to think about how you receive and interpret input from non-sensory sources and how this non-sensory knowledge could be integrated into your ways of thinking.

Central to this new way of thinking is the cultivation of imagination. By defining imagination and showing how important it is to the New Enlightenment, I will show you how this key facet can be used in bringing together both sensory and non-sensory sources of information. The result is that you will learn how you yourself can move beyond the limits of "The Belief" into a new way of thinking and perceiving.

You will also understand what Einstein meant when he said:

A human is a part of the whole called by us, "the universe." Apart, limited in time and space, he experiences himself, his thoughts and feelings, as something separate from the rest— a kind of optical illusion of consciousness. This delusion is a kind of prison for us, restricting us to our personal desires and affection for a few persons nearest to us. Our task must be to free ourselves from this prison by widening the circle of under-standing and compassion to embrace all living creatures and the whole of nature in its beauty.... We shall require a substan-tially new manner of thinking if humanity is to survive.[14]

---

14 Einstein, several attributions of this quotation, but the one most often cited is *New York Post*, Nov. 28, 1972.

Chapter 1

MOVING BEYOND "THE BELIEF"
Introducing the New Enlightenment

"We feel suffocated and don't know why. The existence of a soul is beyond proof under the ruling premises, but people go on behaving as though they had souls, nevertheless. They behave as if they came from another place, another life, and they have impulses and desires that nothing in this world, none of our present premises, can account for."
—Saul Bellow (*Humboldt's Gift*)

In the introduction, you learned of "The Belief," a theory of knowledge that grew out of the European Enlightenment of the eighteenth century and has since become the only realistic and accepted way for Westerners to think. Saul Bellow terms it "the ruling premises," but its meaning is the same. Bellow, in the quotation above, gives a veiled plea for humanity to accept that our impulses and desires may come from broader premises than what may seem possible within the current environment of rigid adherence to the five senses. With this in mind, let's proceed with some new premises. In order to arrive at our goal let's take a look at how we became so entrenched in "The Belief."

The Scientific Method

By the time you take your first science class, often in the fifth grade, "The Belief" has informally shaped you in significant ways. With your first science class, your formal indoctrination begins. Let's follow the story of one of the children in my neighborhood in Arden Hills, Minnesota, a first-ring suburb of Minneapolis/St. Paul.

Anna Hecht, twelve, attends the middle school in Mounds View, Minnesota. Her science class, as is typical of most public middle schools and uses *McGraw-Hill Science* by Richard Moyer et al. In the text of the opening section of the book below, note the connection between the study of the basic particles of matter and the scientific method.

> **Main Idea:** *All matter* (emphasis added) is made of elements.... In studying matter scientists face a challenge. The basic particles that make up matter are too small to be seen directly. In the past the tests scientists performed on matter gave only hints about how matter is put together. That's because particles of matter cannot be observed.... Elements are the basic building blocks of all matter.... In 1803, an English scientist named John Dalton stated an important theory: Matter is made up of tiny particles that cannot be cut apart into smaller pieces. Today we call Dalton's tiny particles atoms.... Atoms are made of protons, neutrons, and electrons.

Pictured next to this text are models of atoms, consisting of neutrons and protons clustered in the middle of a colored sphere, with several electrons whizzing about. Students are asked at the end of the section to "draw a model of a beryllium atom." The text proceeds with a description of the methods of science (see chart on page 3).

The text proceeds to identify certain process skills used by science. Thirteen skills are listed, each with a brief explanation. A sampling of the thirteen are:

> *Observe*—to use one or more of the senses to identify or learn about an object or event
> *Infer*—to form an idea from facts or observations
> *Classify*—to place things that share properties together in groups
> *Predict*—to state possible results of an event or experiment
> *Model*—to make something that represent an object or event (Moyer et al., *Science*)

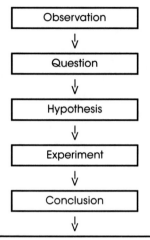

```
┌─────────────────────────────┐
│         Observation         │
└─────────────────────────────┘
               ↓
┌─────────────────────────────┐
│          Question           │
└─────────────────────────────┘
               ↓
┌─────────────────────────────┐
│         Hypothesis          │
└─────────────────────────────┘
               ↓
┌─────────────────────────────┐
│         Experiment          │
└─────────────────────────────┘
               ↓
┌─────────────────────────────┐
│         Conclusion          │
└─────────────────────────────┘
               ↓
```

Results support hypothesis—communicate results
or
Results do not support hypothesis—restart the process

As you can see from the excerpt, Anna learns from the beginning of her formal education that science concerns itself with the study of matter. Implicit within the text is the assumption that science does not study what does not contain matter, such as, for example, honesty, courage, or freedom. At the same time, reinforced over and over throughout the rest of her life, is the belief that science and scientists are the most capable of addressing the tough challenges that face our world.

Science, as presented to Anna in this formal way, has a direct connection to the language she has been learning informally. This informal knowledge of language, learned through interacting with others and reading books, unconsciously teaches many of the principles of logic of science that allow her to easily understand and accept formal teaching about science without questioning it or understanding its limits. Later you will see the direct relationship between language and science, specifically as it relates to the subject/object dichotomy that is at the heart of classical science.

"The Belief":
The Good, the Problematic, the Bad, and the Irony

I have posited that "The Belief" limits our knowledge and suggested that there are other means to gain knowledge. However, I want to emphasize that the thinking underlying "The Belief" has led to unprecedented advancements in technology.

"The Belief": The Good. This simple and ingenious methodological flow has led to inventions such as:

- Electricity and large grids able to provide electrical power across most of the globe
- The integrated mass production of products and infrastructures that provide water, housing, food, and clothing for billions
- Mechanized land and air travel
- Communication devices such as television, phones, and the Internet
- Medical technologies that have saved lives and enhanced the quality of countless others
- Transformative inventions that have widespread application such as transistors, lasers, the light bulb, antibiotics, and the computer chip

Also, one can think of the selfless mobilization of resources (and the appeal to our inner humanity) for the work of building schools for the deaf, establishing medical clinics to treat leprosy in developing countries, the elimination of polio and small pox, the work of Boy and Girl Scouts, the Red Cross, Civil Air Patrol, and countless other organizations; or in the good work done through the financial contributions and research of many of the world's great corporations, religious institutions, and social agencies. All would be impossible but for the advancements brought about by the "The Belief." There are many more examples in virtually every field of study and occupation.

Another remarkable result of Enlightenment thinking concerns our ability to think analytically. Many of modern life's problems are so complex, they could never have been solved without the simplification that is a result of abstract thinking. I will cover abstract thinking in chapter 4 in detail, showing how it evolved in conjunction with Enlightenment thinking as well as showing how it works as a simplifying agent in solving complex problems. Stated simply, we think much differently than people of the past. This understanding will also be an important part of unfolding the New Enlightenment.

The problematic. These wonderful advances brought about by scientific thinking have also produced other, less desirable results. Our Western education system based largely on scientific thinking has concluded that all other ways of thinking are pre-scientific, religious, or superstitious. The assumption is that they are inferior to scientific thinking. Consequently, only scientific thinking receives central focus in public and most private education. This results in "scientism," the worship of the scientific thinking born of "The Belief." Our children, consequently, grow up as we did, thinking that the way we "see" the world is the correct way. Most cannot even conceive of other ways to "see" the world.

Over the past two centuries, as "The Belief" has become entrenched, Western societies have moved to the current position of not granting a platform to other ways of thinking when it relates to matters of public policy. The logic of governments, often unstated, goes as follows:

1. We prefer not to be interested in propositions which cannot be empirically verified
2. All propositions which cannot be empirically verified are essentially meaningless
3. We shall legislate to prevent anyone else wasting his time on meaningless propositions, at least with our money

Our newspapers and television reports operate from this way of thinking. Science has become scientism and has replaced religion, both in running society and in educating its people. Most Westerners now place scientists in the role of advisors regarding how to live and how to solve problems. We may pay attention to pop culture and be interested in all sorts of alternative thought, but when push comes to shove we tend to follow what the scientists tell us as reported to us in the media.

When Anna, the twelve-year-old from Mounds View, becomes an adult, she will digest news reports that reinforce the notion that science and the scientific method alone provide humanity's best hope for addressing societal and global issues. She will pass this way of viewing the world on to her children, and the cycle will reset. "The Belief" is a dominating way to think. But there is a tradeoff in making scientists the priests of our existence.

The Bad. Enlightenment thinking is utilitarian in that it works exceptionally well with the manipulation of the material world. It does not work well in other arenas that require holistic, long-term moral and ethical thinking, such as the environmental impacts of inventions, long-term results of genetic reengineering, and the results of creating various bio-agents. Enlightenment thinking struggles to understand how to deal with the loss of natural habitats for species, since issues surrounding this topic require decisions to be made that deal with morality and the balancing of the needs of varying species.

In addition, Enlightenment thinking does not do well in understanding human interactions, relations, and mutual interdependence. The only help it provides for improving internal psychological difficulties—individual neuroses, depression, estrangement from nature, and existential disappointment—comes from a medicine chest, which alters the symptoms while failing to treat the source of these difficulties.

There are other effects. Disillusionment, serial killing, nuclear weaponry, and biological warfare are all legacies of the Enlightenment. Scientific progress allows for evil to use that technology for genocides, holocausts, and world wars. Likely, humanity cannot continue in the same vein in the twenty-first century or there may be no twenty-second century. There seems to be an abyss between human knowing and human doing.

"The Belief'" also has a number of identifiable, though less-obvious, direct effects.

The belief that we are isolated individual objects. We have lost meaning in life by living within the confines of "The Belief." Many in our society have carried "The Belief" to its logical conclusion: "If we are merely objects, and the only things that are real are made up of matter, then what does life matter?" Many philosophers of the past century declared similar perspectives. Perhaps no clearer example of this philosophy, often termed nihilism, can be found in Albert Camus's *The Stranger*, whose main character committed a murder with no sense of concern for the victim or for his own potential future execution. Readers get a palpable sense of his experience of being cut off from any connection to anything outside of her/his own physical being.

The loss of the meaning of history. For Enlightenment thinkers, everything that has come before is mere curiosity, to be preserved in museums and history texts, or as fodder for historical novels. History is turned into facts and dates and away from understanding previous ways of thinking and living. These previous ways of living and thinking are not viewed as important for today, when there is considerable lost or forgotten wisdom that we need in order to navigate the millennium ahead.

The creation of idols and modern society's entrenched sin of literalness. We idolize objects such as money and tangible property when we don't even know how our minds are complicit in creating the very things we strive to obtain. We are literalists when it comes to physical objects and property. No wonder fights over money, property, and land feel like life and death struggles.

Hyper-consumer culture. The materialistic emphasis of "The Belief" leads to unbalanced lifestyles with addictions to technologies.

Ignorance of the effects of words and language. We are not taught about the power of words and language. Words and language directly affect what we think about and what we ignore in our world. In order to handle our world's problems we must bring light to their power.

The danger of collectivity without individual freedom. At first glance this seems contradictory since the Enlightenment age is truly the age of the individual. Ironically, however, the loss of meaning that results from "The Belief" leads to a vacuum of moral leadership which opens the door for dominant power spheres to emerge, such as Hitler's Germany, Communist Russia, and Cambodia's Khmer Rouge. In these regimes, individual thought was suppressed while impulses for morality were quelled. Currently our world struggles to handle the potential emergence of powerful ultra-religious fundamentalism.

The disenchantment and objectifying of nature. Given that nature is nothing but a collection of objects, so the thinking goes, we should dominate and subdue it. We do not see our connection to nature, so it makes sense that we manipulate nature for our own short-term ends.

Heightened numbers of depressed, anxious, drug-addicted individuals.[1] This ties directly to the loss of meaning in life and the belief that we are existentially alone in the world.

The loss of awe we had as children. For example, small children are fascinated with seeing light emerge in a dark room or watching lightning in the sky. This sense of awe is quickly squelched by the logical philosophies that are the unwitting outcomes of the hegemony of "The Belief." How does one learn about light in our Western universities other than by taking classes that, through the use of mathematical formulae, show how light involves particles and waves? This reduction of light to math removes any other type of knowledge of light.[2]

Finally, "The Belief" has no answer for Socrates' question, "How should I live?" Science has not developed any system of ethics or

---

1   This is discussed more fully in the next subsection.

2   See Zajonc, *Catching the Light: The Entwined History of Light and Mind.*

wisdom, unless one considers Friedrich Nietzsche's nihilistic philosophy. He believed Western society to be flawed with its foundation on the unstable Enlightenment. He predicted the collapse of meaning brought about by nihilism as the most destructive force in history.[3] Nobel Prize–winning quantum physicist Erwin Schrödinger stated:

> The image of the world around us that science provides is highly deficient. It supplies a lot of factual information, and puts all our experience in magnificently coherent order, but keeps terribly silent about everything close to our hearts, everything that really counts for us."[4]

As such, "The Belief" serves as an ideal environment to produce a rise in radical fundamentalism as a counter to the nihilism of the scientific worldview.

My point in showing the limits of, and negative effects resulting from, "The Belief" is to show that, as a system of knowledge, it was never intended to answer all of life's questions concerning the issues of meaning. Yet it has become so for much of Western society. Making it the center of our education system, and the only generally *agreed-upon* way of coming to knowledge of anything, has led to the woes listed above.

The Irony. Advances in technology have led physicists to recognize that "The Belief" cannot be the end-all answer, yet they continue to live as if it is the truth, the whole truth, and nothing but the truth. Consider the following Newtonian laws: It is presumed that the basic "building blocks" of the material world (atoms, molecules, quarks) are "dead" and therefore without inner reality, subjectivity, feelings, perception, experience, self-causation, and meaning.[5] In accordance with their deadness, wouldn't it be true that these inert building blocks of matter—fundamental to the world we experience—can only be moved from one location to another by other

---

3   Nietzsche, *The Will to Power.*

4   Quoted in, Revel and Ricard, *The Monk and the Philosopher.*

5   Searle, *Consciousness and Language.*

objects, via contact from another object or material-based energy source? "The Belief" would answer that abstract question with a resounding "yes." But physicists discovered long ago the quantum field is a trove of linear contradiction. When broken down to its fundamental elements, subatomic particles do not behave as we expect matter to behave and, indeed, appear to move from one location to the next without any known catalyzing event.

Physicists know this is a logical fallacy that "The Belief" cannot harmonize. "The Belief" is premised on the fact that "dead" material can only be moved through a physical "touching" of other matter, yet that simply is not the case with subatomic particles. The phrase "building blocks of the material world," which appears in virtually all basic science books, including Anna's fifth-grade text, implies that the world has been built brick by brick from its smallest unit of matter—yet how can this be so if these microscopic "dead" particles appear to "show up" at a given location at random? So many Westerners, including those of most every religious persuasion, accept "The Belief" without thinking, because we've been taught from the beginning of our education to believe it is true. Even as physicists have learned that there might be something more to subatomic particles that "The Belief" cannot answer, they are so unconscious of the effects of our Enlightenment worldview that they continue to live as if "The Belief" is true.

Western Philosophies and the Increase in Mental Illness

One of the negative results of "The Belief" deserves more expansion. Mental illnesses are increasingly pervasive in Western societies. Determining why such dramatic numbers of people are afflicted with these illnesses is a daunting task but can be explained at least in part due to the cognitive framework of "The Belief" and the resultant philosophies embraced by Westerners.

In its annual report on the state of mental and physical health of citizens of the United States, the National Institute of Health reported that Major Depressive Disorder is the leading cause of disability in the US for ages fifteen to forty-four.[6] It affects approximately 14.8 million American adults, or about 6.7 percent of the U.S. population age eighteen and older in a given year[7] and is more prevalent in women than in men. They also report that anxiety disorders affect approximately forty million American adults ages eighteen and older (i.e., about 18.1 percent of people in this age group in a given year have an anxiety disorder). Anxiety disorders include panic disorder, obsessive-compulsive disorder, post-traumatic stress disorder, generalized anxiety disorder, and phobias (social phobia, agoraphobia, and specific phobia). They frequently co-occur with depressive disorders or substance abuse.

In addition, approximately six million American adults ages eighteen and older, or about 2.7 percent of people in this age group in a given year, have panic disorder. These typically develop in early adulthood (median age of onset is twenty-four), but the age of onset extends throughout adulthood. About one in three people with panic disorder develops agoraphobia, a condition in which the individual becomes afraid of being in any place or situation where escape might be difficult or help might be unavailable in the event of a panic attack.[8]

Ethan Watters, in addressing these issues in his book *Crazy Like Us,* has gone so far as to suggest that as we introduce Americanized ways of treating mental illnesses, we are in fact spreading the diseases.[9] He cites our hyper-individualism as the culprit. He describes this hyper-individualism as the idea that the individual

---

6   "The global burden of disease: 2004 update, Table A2: Burden of disease in DALYs by cause, sex and income group in WHO regions, estimates for 2004" (*The World Health Organization,* 2008).

7   Kessler, et al., "Prevalence, Severity, and Co-morbidity of Twelve-month DSM-IV disorders in the national comorbidity survey replication (NCS-R)" (*Archives of General Psychiatry,* 2005 Jun 62(6):617–27). "U.S. Census Bureau Population Estimates by Demographic Characteristics. Table 2: Annual Estimates of the Population by Selected Age Groups and Sex for the United States: Apr. 1, 2000 to July 1, 2004 (NC-EST2004-02)" Population Division, U.S. Census Bureau: Release Date, June 9, 2005.

8   Kessler, et al., "Prevalence, Severity, and Co-morbidity..."

9   Watters, *Crazy Like Us.*

has little need for social groupings. I believe he has identified the issue and its effects, though his work does not discuss how hyper-individualism evolved to become predominant in America, something you will learn as you continue reading this book.

Another troubling and under-reported aspect of our current situation concerns the number of suicides. MIT Senior Lecturer Otto Scharmer reports that three times as many people worldwide take their own lives than people who take others' lives in all the wars and murders combined.

Such widespread affliction of suicides and mental illnesses can be traced to the logical outcomes flowing from the Western adherence to two basic philosophies: dualism and materialism (also called realism or natural philosophy). These philosophies, embraced by everyone from atheists, religious fundamentalists, traditional Christians (Catholic, Lutheran, Presbyterian), Muslims, and Jews, are the result of hundreds of years of adhering to "The Belief." In order to understand more of how "The Belief" has us in a straitjacket we will examine these philosophies a bit more deeply.

Dualism and Materialism. According to "The Belief" one can trust the knowledge concerning matter that is obtained through the rigors of scientific methods. Both dualism and materialism agree that matter exists; it is real and science can uncover knowledge of matter. The main difference between these two dominant modern philosophies concerns the role of "mind" and its contribution to experiencing the world. Dualism asserts that human minds exist and are substantively different than the body; that is, there are two separate and distinct "substances" of the universe—mind and matter, and minds are not made up of matter. For most dualists, what occurs in the mind includes thoughts and experiences, which involve a duration, or extension, in time. Any experience of which we are aware occurs in our mind. Dualists believe that the mind's experience of time is a "real" event.

Dualists and materialists both believe that matter is "real" and exists as measurable extensions in space—i.e., even a microscopic object takes up (extends into) space. However, dualists struggle to talk about any interaction between mind and matter. They conclude by saying that the mind is the "ghost in the machine" that does not affect the machine, or if it does, it affects the machine much less than the machine affects it. This is, in essence, the result of René Descartes's well-known *cogito ergo sum,* "I think, therefore I am," statement. Western religions tend to be dualistic, at least in practice. I find, however, that dualists have a difficult time gaining access to the public square. Given that reality, and given that dualists operate with essentially the same theory of knowledge as materialists (this will become clearer in the pages ahead), I will focus most of my comments on the materialist manifestation of the Enlightenment.

Materialists are generally atheists or agnostics. They assert that, although we believe or feel that our minds are separate from our body, this belief or feeling is merely the result of the matter in our brain interacting and producing it. This belief, termed monistic physicalism, explains that the experiences of the mind (emotions, thoughts, perceptions, volitions) occur because of the way the physical brain has evolved and been configured. One materialist interpretation explains these experiences of the mind by referring to them as evolution's new *emergent properties,* drawing a parallel to what occurred in eons past in the emergences of bones, lungs, and skin.

What is an Experience? What materialists overlook, however, is that these experiences of the mind are just that, experiences. They are not like objects such as bones and skin that can be examined. They are interior to a mind and, by definition, cannot be the object of observation by our five senses. One cannot take an experience out of one's mind and examine it as a thing.

As New York University professor Thomas Nagel notes in his essay "What Is It Like to Be a Bat?":

> The fact that an organism has conscious experience at all
> means basically, that there is something it is like to be that
> organism.... We may call this the subjective character of
> experience. It is not captured by any of the familiar, recently

devised reductive analyses of the mental, for all of them are logically compatible with its absence.[10]

It is ironic that, as materialists trust their experiences of observing, analyzing, and drawing conclusions concerning matter, they base their trust on something that cannot be examined. According to their assertion, a mind is simply a fantasy. That's a rather huge fly in their logical soup.

Do we want engineers only? For materialists, knowledge consists of seeing what happens and getting used to it. Barfield illustrates a problem with this view of the universe by analogizing it to an automobile. Materialists satisfy themselves with how the internal combustion of a vehicle works by entering the vehicle, pulling all the visible levers, and watching what happens. Inevitably, pulling the levers leads to some sort of acceleration. Materialists then conclude that their "actions" show the "meaning" of the vehicle (universe), or they conclude that a discussion of meaning is irrelevant. In reality they compulsively pull levers and push buttons but have no idea what is happening under the hood.[11] We will spend much of our time looking under the hood in the pages that follow.

Outcomes of Western Philosophies. One logical outcome that arises from a starting point of materialism and dualism has been termed *causal determinism.*[12] This means that the present material state of affairs has been completely and wholly determined by what happened previously, which in turn was determined by what happened previously, and so on. Any observed evolution is a mindless consequence of the mechanism that was turned on by the Big Bang theory of the origin of the universe. What we

---

10   Nagel, "What is it like to be a bat?" (*The Philosophical Review*, October 1974, LXXXIII:[4]:435–450).

11   Barfield, *Poetic Diction.*

12   Briefly discussed, though not named, in the section above titled "The Irony"

experience as life, therefore, is a random mechanical process that is fundamentally without meaning.

Lack of meaning likely has a profound impact on mental illness, though this assertion has yet to be empirically tested. Viktor Frankl and Salvatore Maddi have suggested a strong correlation between a lack of meaning and purpose in life.[13] According to a recent article describing research around boredom, depression, and meaning, the minimal empirical research that has been conducted suggests that meaning, boredom, and depression are strongly and significantly inter-correlated. Furthermore, the relation between boredom and depression appears to be driven by meaning.[14]

Another logical outcome from the basic premises of materialism and dualism, and common to both philosophies, is *reductionism*. Reductionism is the belief that everything is reducible to its parts, and that any apparently purposeful actions are reducible to mechanics. This, along with causal determinism, requires science to limit itself to investigating and making statements regarding merely the behavior of things. No discussion of meaning or purpose or intention is testable and, consequently, cannot be assumed to have any causal significance. Nature, in order to be studied in this way, must be "mathematized." That means it must be made amenable to quantitative studies that require it to be broken down to its constituent parts and analyzed. Though you can gain many insights this way, you lose all the insights that come from viewing the living entity in its living environment.

Without a connection outside of one's own individuality, as I stated previously, history is fundamentally meaningless and life consists merely of "one damn thing after another,"[15] resulting in depression, illness, withdrawal, or indulgence. This results

---

13 Frankl, *Man's Search for Meaning* and *The Unheard Cry for Meaning*; Maddi, "The existential neurosis" (*Journal of Abnormal Psychology*: 1967, 72:311–325); and "The Search for Meaning," in Arnold & Page, *The Nebraska Symposium on Motivation*, pp. 134–183.

14 Fahlman et al., "Does a Lack of Meaning in Life Cause Boredom and Depression?" http://www.meaning.ca/archives/archive/art_meaning_boredom _dpression_S_Fahlman.html (Toronto: York University).

15 Barfield, *History, Guilt, and Habit.*

directly from our sense of being "cut off." Philosophy calls this experience *existentialism*.

Existentialists have been seduced by "The Belief" into believing in the absence of significant external reality. For them, the presence of human freedom carries with it the heavy burden of responsibility for this freedom. Not recognizing "the roots of human freedom in the whole evolution of human consciousness, they feel crushed by the weight."[16] They claim that individuals are responsible for all that exists, but do not acknowledge an "inside" or internal meaning to this crushing weight.

Yet another logical conclusion of "The Belief" is the assumption that all perception is limited to what can be perceived by the senses. With that as an assumption, it follows then that the only experiences that can be intelligently discussed by educated people are those experiences that are a feature of our human central nervous system and sensory organs (or accessible through these senses and any extension of them via technology). This conclusion eliminates any consideration of communication from non-material sources. Humanity is left again to view the material world as "all there is" and seems to further disconnect humanity from "meaning" that could come from a non-material source.

Does All Science and Research Continually Build and Improve on the Past? In tandem with "The Belief" most Westerners believe that all contemporary researchers in all fields of study are "better" and more accurate than those of previous years. A simple result of this naïve thinking is the assumption that a university class, Sociology 101 for example, taken in 2011 is by definition "better" than one taken in 1978. It is also said anecdotally that throughout a four-year course of study in psychology, what a student learns their freshman year is outdated knowledge by the time they graduate.

This assumption coincides with the belief that young researchers advance a field of study with new research and discoveries that build

---

16   Barfield, *Worlds Apart.*

on previous thought-leaders in their disciplines. These advancements are assumed to take place in both physical and biological sciences as well as in social sciences (such as education, political science, anthropology, sociology, and the like). In many cases these assumptions of "advancement" are unwarranted, since building on a flawed assumption only perpetuates the flaw. Unfortunately, as ideas and approaches gain momentum, whether they are built on flawed assumptions or not, they attract grants, which in turn attract more researchers. Universities wishing to capitalize on the interest in the "new," and assumed better, approach of a field will endow a faculty chair to enhance the propagation of the approach, all resulting in the assumption being made by non-experts that this approach is the "state-of-the-art" for the discipline of study. This process has certainly been played out in Western societies for those who espouse deterministic and materialistic assumptions.

Glimmers of Something beyond "The Belief"

Many of you may already have experiences of other means to knowledge than those resulting from that gained by scientific thinking alone. You may, for example, be of strong religious faith and have seen dramatic changes in the lives of individuals who were once self-destructive and who, subsequently, turned their lives around with the help of non-material teachings of a church, mosque, synagogue, temple, or other religious gathering place. You recognize that an immaterial source helped the individual, though you don't understand how it works.

Others, whether from your knowledge of popularized quantum physics and its astounding implications,[17] from the writings of physicists such as David Bohm, from an interest in Eastern thought, or from an increased understanding of mind–body medicine, also see possibilities beyond "The Belief." As well, you may have been intrigued by events you have experienced, or stories described by others, using mind–body medicine, experiencing synchronous natural

---

17   Arntz et al., *What the Bleep Do We Know?*

phenomenon,[18] or non-local communication (e.g., dogs responding to masters' intentions halfway around the world, the telepathic parrot, and other groundbreaking studies of Rupert Sheldrake[19]).

But you have been poured into a mold by "The Belief" and, though for a time you feel a sense of amazement at these ideas and experiences, you don't know what to do with them. Consequently, either you live in contradiction and uncertainty or you don't think too much about them. "The Belief" is a mold from which it is hard to break free. I've struggled against the mold for many years and am still working on it.

Summary

We've taken some time to look at "The Belief" and its effects in our world. However, no matter how incisive a critique, it is difficult to give up a way of doing something that is comfortable and known and has produced so much obvious good (along with the negative). From talking with many people over the years, I've learned that it can be helpful, perhaps even necessary, to show the flaw inherent in "The Belief" born from using the scientific method. This makes it easier for individuals to be open to other means of thought that can supersede the flaw once it is seen. To accomplish this we will look at the flaw, science's Trojan Horse, in the next chapter.

---

18 See http://www.nps.gov/grsm/naturescience/fireflies.htm.

19 Sheldrake, *Dogs that Know When Their Owners Are Coming Home.*

Chapter 2

THE TROJAN HORSE OF SCIENCE

"We are only at the beginning of the development of the human race; of the development of the human mind, of intelligent life.... It is our responsibility not to give the answer today as to what it is all about, to drive everybody down in that direction and to say: 'This is a solution to it all.' Because we will be chained then to the limits of our present imagination."
—RICHARD FEYNMAN (*The Pleasure of Finding Things Out*)

Virgil's *Aeneid* tells the story of The Trojan Horse. As the story goes, the city of Troy has been under siege for more than ten years. The Greeks, outside the city's fortress walls and unable to gain access, build a huge wooden horse and pretend to sail away. The Trojans, believing the Greeks have given up and left, bring the horse inside their gates and celebrate their victory. Inside the horse, thirty Greek men are hiding. In the middle of the night the men leave the horse and open the gates. The Greek army, which had returned, enters the city, wins the war, and assimilates the Trojans into their empire.

Like Troy, the scientific method has its own Trojan Horse invited in by science itself. This Trojan Horse, when it is revealed more widely in society (many scientists are quite aware of it), will be instrumental in opening the gate to a better science that will incorporate and greatly surpass current science. But before we can get to that part of the story we must understand the Horse, which consists of ideas inherent in the scientific method. We begin with two of the foundational premises of the scientific method:

Premise 1: There is mind; there is matter. The two are
completely unrelated
Premise 2: Science, in order to be objective, determines to
study matter, not mind, since mind is not knowable by the
scientific method

With these premises in mind, let's now return to the logic of the
scientific method, as presented in the previous chapter, and expand
our statements about it.

- Ask a question—The question must be about something
objective, something that can be tested and measured
- Do background research—Learn relevant scientific "facts"
about the issue on which you are focused
- Construct a hypothesis—Use your mind and/or your
imagination to create a hypothesis. Seek to discover what is
objectively inherent in whatever you are studying or testing
- Test your hypothesis—Use investigative methods such as
experiments, comparisons, descriptions, or models, to validate or invalidate your hypothesis
- Analyze your data and draw a conclusion—Use logic and
reason to report what the investigation discovered
- Repeat—If necessary, investigate the question in a different way or at a different time or place to demonstrate the
dependability of the first investigation
- Communicate your results—Publish an article or study stating your conclusion. You receive credit for thinking of the
hypothesis, but you understand that what your investigation demonstrates is resident within matter, unaffected by
you. You've simply discovered what is already there

This has been the typical pattern used by science for centuries
and has produced the great results I briefly listed in the previous
chapter and continues to produce great results. It has also resulted
in science discovering the limits beyond which it cannot proceed. A
very brief history will highlight this discovery.

Descartes and the Search for the Fundamental Particle

During the seventeenth century, Descartes was the first prominent philosopher to formulate the chasm between matter (objects)
and mind (subjects) as a philosophical principle with his famous "I
think; therefore, I am." The methods of natural science are erected
on that principle, which proceeds as follows: *If you want to know
about "things," or the material world in which we live, you must
only study the "things." You cannot study the mind.* Nor can you
study the human psyche or human values, only the corresponding
physical state of the brain.

Science followed Descartes's principle and made a distinction
between the primary and secondary, or "occult,"[1] qualities of matter.
Primary qualities, the ones that they determined can be studied by science—e.g., the things that are "really there"—are extensions in space,
solidity, figure, and motion. These are qualities, they concluded, that
can be expressed mathematically. Physicists of the seventeenth and
eighteenth centuries endeavored to study these qualities and to omit
any secondary qualities. Secondary qualities, they asserted, are those
influenced by the human mind, such as color, sound, and taste. These
were deemed to be "subjective" since they are generally incapable of
being expressed mathematically. Science's goal in dealing with secondary qualities was to find the mechanism at work behind them, a
mechanism they assumed could be expressed mathematically.

By the primary quality of space these philosophers meant the
three dimensions of our physical reality—the length, width, and
height taken up by objects. By solidity they meant that every object
consists of some form of matter, regardless of how small the matter
may turn out to be. By figure they meant that objects take a shape
and form, even if these change frequently or rapidly. And by motion
they meant any sort of movement in time.

Their identification of these primary qualities seems to make
perfect sense—*if* you believe in an objective world, separate from

---

1   Nothing pejorative or mysterious is meant by the use of the term *occult*; it
     simply refers to something "hidden."

the human mind. Essentially, primary qualities were believed to be *independent of human sensory organs.*[2] The Classical Newtonian physics of this era assumed that all secondary qualities were based on movement and consequently were not interested in these secondary qualities. They wanted to discover the basic matter, the "stuff" upon which everything depended and was erected. They expected to find some stable, static substance, microscopic though it may be. In so doing they would express this "stuff" mathematically since science assumed that doing so was more "real" than any experience of secondary qualities—these movable, imprecise, slippery, subjective experiences.

"Occult" Qualities. Secondary qualities—color, odor, smell, and the like—cannot be scientifically measured, or mathematized, since they are results of human sensory organs and their interactions with primary qualities. Barfield explains it this way:

> It was by the rigorous exclusion from its field, under the name of "occult qualities," of every element, whether spiritual or mental or called by any other name, which can only be conceived as non-material, and therefore non-measurable, that natural knowledge acquired a precision unknown before...armed with that precision (entitling it to the name of "science"), went on to achieve its formidable technological victories. It is the elimination of occult qualities from the purview of science that constitutes the difference between astrology and astronomy, between alchemy and chemistry, and in general the difference between Aristotelian man and his environment in the past and modern man and his environment in the present.[3]

These secondary qualities were viewed as "occult," or hidden, from the true knowing revealed by the scientific method. As an

2   The key difference between Enlightenment thinking and New Enlightenment thinking is that, while the former believes in an objective world separate from the human mind, the latter believes mind interpenetrates and creates the world around us and thus cannot be separated.

3   Barfield, "The Case for Anthroposophy" introduction to Steiner, *Riddles of the Soul.*

example, the color "purple" is a quality that cannot be an appropriate focus of science, at least not as it relates to its "purpleness." It appears to our eyes as purple because of its interaction with our eyes and the refraction of light. Eighteenth century scientists would not make determinations regarding purple. But eventually science did determine what "purpleness" meant—i.e., what humans generally see as the color purple is electromagnetic radiation with a wavelength of around 400 nanometers. In this respect one can see how science mathematized purple and thus reduced it to a quantity.

For science of the seventeenth and eighteenth centuries, in essence, it does not matter if "mind," or psyche, exists or not. It became inevitable that science would study only that which science could show as being devoid of psyche. Once the material world has been affirmed to be completely independent of psyche, it does not matter if psyche exists or not. There is no need to deny its existence or affirm it, since by definition it is occult and cannot be an object of study. It might as well not be there.

Monistic Physicalism. The science of the Enlightenment era established its core premises and constructed means of investigation that adhered only to those premises. Any issues regarding mind or psyche were believed to be either incapable of being investigated and, consequently, not a part of the work of the scientific community, or to be explainable through the purely physical.

Many went so far as to propose a monistic physicalism (see also p. 13), meaning that only matter is real (hence the word monistic), mind does not exist, and that there are no bona fide mental events. These theorists have long hoped for the discovery of a fundamental particle, the basic "stuff" of the universe. Through this discovery they could then explain all of what are termed "mental events" in purely physical terms, such as brain states producing such experiences as color or pain.

What Is Really "There"? As science entered the nineteenth century, optimism raged regarding the hoped-for discovery of the secrets of nature and the discovery of the fundamental stable stuff of the universe. However, when scientists in physics, neurology, and the other sciences investigated the core building blocks of all matter, they found something they did not expect. While looking for a basic particle smaller than a grain of sand, they realized that the supposed particles are microscopic, and even submicroscopic.

The Quandary of Quantum Physics

As research moved ever deeper, they discovered a dramatic gulf between atomic structure and what we experience as the familiar world of objects, energy, nature, and ourselves. This produced a quandary.

Lots of Empty Space. Twentieth century probing into the subatomic world revealed what our minds struggle to understand. They discovered, for example, that what we refer to as an atom consists primarily of empty space, so much so that were an atom blown up to the size of a city block, its protons and neutrons would each be the size of a grain of sand, and the electrons would not be there, "showing up" only when we looked for them. Also, prior to showing up, quantum physics assures us, the electron wasn't actually anywhere in our known universe but either somewhere else or, even more amazing, everywhere at the same time. The rest of the atom is *empty.* Our familiar world is simply incongruent with the world physicists tell us is "real."

Constant Transformation. Along with this unsettling description of "matter" at its smallest form, we are told that, at the quantum level, whatever material we expect to be able to identify we cannot actually locate. All of the quantum "material" appears to be incessantly transforming—a sort of quantum shapeshifting. Particles become waves which become particles seemingly at random. Quantum physicists tell us the mass of these "particles" is zero. At the quantum level nothing is stable, and no substance has been discovered as the root of all matter.

Concerning these waves, physicists assure us that the waves not only have no mass, they have no structure, and do not take up space. These waves are said to be energies distributed equally throughout the universe; sort of "smeared" everywhere. Because of this discovery, physicists have had to revise the whole notion of space, since Newtonian physics had always asserted that the existence of a body requires it to be localized in some definite region of space. To give an example that summarizes quantum science discoveries concerning matter, the table in front of me takes up "space," but when the "material" that makes up the table is analyzed on a subatomic level, it does not take up space and is not "there"—*until it is looked for by a researcher.* Then, the subatomic particles show up.

This leads some to question whether there is a negative or potential space, that at the subatomic level the particles are waiting to emerge from another dimension, one of potentiality. Perhaps the elementary particle science has long sought might be conceived, not as a tiny bit of matter but as the detectable moment of transition from structure or potential structure in negative space to ordinary inner structure in Newtonian space. Which leads us to a key question: What, if any, is the role of thought in this since quantum physics posits that *mind co-creates matter*?

If you are confused you are not alone. Our minds struggle to grasp the meaning of these discoveries. Help comes when we start our investigations not with matter itself, but with our minds and how they come to "know" something. In order to begin looking at how our minds work, let's consider the role of mental concepts.

Mediated by Concepts. Biologist Marjorie Grene[4] and coauthor David Depew wrote the first history of the philosophy of biology. In it, they said that the world, as we experience it, is "mediated by concepts as well as presented through the senses."[5] Most

---

4   In 2002, she was the first female philosopher to have an edition of the "Library of Living Philosophers" written about her.

5   Grene, *The Knower and the Known.*

Westerners can understand that the world we experience appears the way it appears due to how it filters through our senses. However, when Grene and Depew say that the world is "mediated by concepts," they mean that the world we experience comes about through the interpenetration of sensory data and the concepts in our minds. This was a radical challenge to traditional science as it allowed for a central role to be played by the human mind.

We have all been educated to believe that matter is "real," that nature is a process governed by impersonal laws, and that objects exist objectively without us. In other words, most of us believe our world is just a machine that would go on impersonally with or without our presence on the planet. Grene and Depew and modern day quantum physicists say otherwise—that the world we "know" would cease to exist without the way our minds interpenetrate with sensory data.

Ironically, however, most of these physicists also struggle to understand what they have discovered. They continue, along with most of Western society, to be unwitting victims of "The Belief." Despite theorizing the role played by the concepts of our minds in shaping the external world, they continue to discuss the topic from a materialistic perspective. It is as if they do not have the vocabulary to work with that would allow them to begin with the human mind and how it knows. Were they to begin with the human mind, the starting point of the theory of knowledge of the New Enlightenment, they would have a much better way to see and understand the phenomena they are studying. But it requires a completely different way of "seeing." Before we proceed to that part of our journey, however, let's conclude this look at the move of science during the last one hundred years.

No More Causation

Scientists in the twentieth century have discovered mistakes in other "laws" entrenched from the Enlightenment. Since the time of Isaac Newton, the laws of cause and effect and of inertia have been at the foundation of scientific theory. The laws are summarized in the following statements:

1. The behavior of an entity (any physical object, phenomenon, situation, or event) depends on its interaction with another entity
2. The cause must be prior to, or at least simultaneous with, the effect
3. The cause and effect must be in spatial (physical) contact or connected by a chain of intermediate (physical) contact points

This foundation came under dispute in 1926, when Max Born studied the collision of an electron with a particle. He demonstrated that the result could not be determined exactly, only probabilistically. This became the basis of quantum theory, which, over the course of many subsequent investigations, has forced physicists to abandon these assumptions as they relate to the subatomic world. Physicists using laser spectroscopy have shown, for example, that if twin photons are separated, no matter by how far in terms of distance in space, a change in one creates a simultaneous change in the other, an effect first anticipated by Einstein.

Also, studies of synchronous effects, such as the well-known fireflies of the Smoky Mountains and Southeast Asia,[6] present evidence of phenomena that do not follow the law of cause and effect. These studies and others have resulted in many scientists seeking for theoretical groundings, founded in quantum theory, fractal geometry, and chaos theory. What appears to us as the separation and isolation of objects from each other is, at a deeper level, interconnected. Certainly there is worthy debate as to whether the interconnection is "physical" or non-physical, or some combination of the two, questions that will be treated in due course.

---

6   Long thought to be an exclusively Southeast Asian phenomenon, the dazzling behavior was only discovered in an American firefly species in 1992. One description of the Elkmont, Tennessee, annual event states, "They begin in mid-June at 10 p.m. nightly. They exhibit six seconds of total darkness; then in perfect synchrony, thousands light up six rapid times in a three-second period before all going dark for six more seconds" (http://jayssouth.com /tennessee/fireflies/).

Heisenberg's Uncertainty Principle. One striking aspect of the difference between classical Newtonian physics and quantum physics concerns preciseness. Classical mechanics presupposes that exact measurements can be given to all physical quantities, assuming there are capable measuring devices. In other words, every *thing* has weight, mass, position, momentum, and volume. Quantum mechanics denies this possibility. The prime example of this concerns the position and momentum of a particle. According to quantum mechanics, the more precisely the position of a particle is given, the less precisely can one say what its momentum is.

Also, quantum mechanics does not assume or assert that an unobserved object definitely consists of waves or particles. The appearance of the object as either waves or particles occurs when the experimenter chooses what to observe in a given experiment. By choosing either the wave or the particle picture, the experimenter disturbs untouched nature. Such favoritism unleashes a limitation in what one can learn about nature "as it really is." According to Werner Heisenberg, "Neither atoms, nor even subatomic particles, are real. They form a world of potentialities or possibilities rather than of objects or facts."[7]

"Brain States." Many following Newtonian physics have sought to explain human consciousness through research into "brain states." They purport to show how specific brain states cause the human to experience certain levels of consciousness such as sleeping, or experiencing certain emotions such as laughter or calmness. They describe brain states as involving a "recipe" of sorts, including certain chemical reactions, hormone releases, and neuron/synapse placement and interaction. This physiological material approach leads some to conclude that what we think is funny or sad, beautiful or ugly, silly or meaningful, has a clear material explanation— i.e. "Your brain is in that state at the time you are experiencing x, y, z, and causes you to have such and such experience."

---

7   Quoted in, Revel and Ricard, *The Monk and the Philosopher.*

Jeffrey M. Schwartz and Sharon Begley, in their reports concerning their work with those afflicted with obsessive-compulsive disorder (OCD), present research showing non-material causes. Their cognitive-therapy work demonstrates that, by following their mental processes, patients can produce measurable brain changes (as shown on PET scans) and can dramatically improve their condition. This means their brains physically change shape and size. Remarkably, it appears that those who *want* to improve the most and work the hardest to do so have the best results, as if they will themselves to better health.

For those with OCD who desired to improve, where did their desire to improve originate? Did it come from a brain state of which they are passive conduits? Is their desire some illusion of free will? Are our genes merely passive receptors that evolve and grow in response to our environment? Are we to reduce all human will, morality, and emotion to the interaction of matter? How does all of this fit with quantum theory? Quantum theory does not answer these questions since it relegates these types of questions outside its jurisdiction. But quantum physics has answered questions concerning "objective science." We are now, therefore, able to identify the flaw in the premises at the beginning of this chapter.

The Trojan Horse—We Are Not Passive

The flaw is that any study of the macroscopic world (the familiar world of objects we experience through our senses) is mediated by both concepts and the five senses. In other words, the flaw is assuming that mind and matter are not interrelated. How can you claim to study the familiar world objectively, given that quantum physics has demonstrated that your mind influences—and in fact may "create"— how you "see" the very objects you are claiming to study?

We participate fully in the creation of what we experience through our senses. We are not passive observers. The notion that macroscopic nature exists independently of humanity has been abandoned by all specialists concerned in any way with perception. Physicists, cognitive scientists, and psychologists agree that the objects we perceive and experience are effects or constructs of human individuals.[8] If humans disappeared from Earth, the world as we know it would cease to exist.

Furthermore, the Trojan horse shows that, as science followed the scientific method in studying the subatomic world, it defined the very limits of the scientific method itself. Scientists learned that there is no such thing as objectivity (the basic assumption of classic physics) in the quantum, subatomic realm. Nor is there any stable physical substance at the foundation of the world as we experience it. Heisenberg can be paraphrased this way: "The constant pursuit of classic physics forced a transformation in the very basis of physics."[9] Sir Arthur Eddington, colleague and collaborator with Einstein said this about the Trojan Horse, "The stuff of the world is mind stuff."[10]

To summarize the preceding. As the twentieth century progressed, the physical sciences realized that matter, as we experience it macroscopically, is an interpenetration between mind-created perceptions/concepts and subatomic particles (the only real matter that exists). What we thought we were studying objectively is not, in fact, objective. About the only thing left that Enlightenment science can do objectively is count, since any statement made by quantum physics regarding the mind or matter consists of mathematical equations displaying the probabilities and statistical averages of occurrence X or occurrence Y. In other words, according to quantum science, ours is a world of pure contingency.

Science's Two Premises Are No More. Premise #1 above stated that "There is mind; there is matter. The two are completely unrelated." This premise is no more because matter turns out to be something completely alien to what Enlightenment science expected. What people experience as matter is, in fact, something that comes from how our five senses and our mind interact. Matter, as we see it, is created by our minds.

---

8   Barfield, "Self and Reality," in *The Rediscovery of Meaning and Other Essays.*

9   Heisenberg, *Physics and Philosophy.*

10 Eddington, *The Nature of the Physical World.*

Premise #2 stated that science, in order to be objective, determines to study matter, not mind. Quantum investigations demonstrate that the objective/subjective divide does not hold at a quantum level. Science, in determining to study only what can be objectively verified, ironically used its "objective" methods to prove that objectivity as a principle is in fact unreliable—quantum physics has turned Newtonian physics on its head!

The transformation from the classic physics of Newton to quantum physics has been a function of the qualitative. Science is now in the same place as it was in the seventeenth and eighteenth century when it determined not to study qualities. It turns out everything is qualitative. The Classicists were seeking stable entities, but they discovered that everything is in a constant state of transformation. The search for the fundamental stable entity has been abandoned. The study of causation as an explanatory system has been abandoned in favor of probabilities. The whole study of transformation has now been taken away from science. What's left for physicists today is mathematics on a curve.

Furthermore, science and its materialistic paradigm is no closer today than it was a hundred years ago in solving the problem of human consciousness.[11] According to a materialistic perspective, our individual consciousness is a tiny bit of the world stuck within our body and brain. But how did this consciousness emerge? What has caused it? How can we attempt to explain "consciousness" as we might explain what a wooden table is? Science's means of explanation have failed miserably in excavating consciousness. Science's basic problem is that every attempt at an explanation must begin with forming thoughts about the phenomena of the world. Then you have two different sets of facts—the material world and thoughts about it. For a deeper explanation of the ineffectiveness of science's method regarding consciousness, I refer you to the writings of Daniel Robinson.[12]

---

11   A statement made on numerous occasions by Daniel Robinson, professor
       emeritus, Georgetown University, professor at Oxford University, and author
       of more than forty books on philosophy; see in particular *Consciousness and
       Mental Life* and *The Mind.*

12   Robinson, *Consciousness and Mental Life*

Thankfully, this is not the whole story. Science is far from dead. However, it needs to discover its soul. The problem with the materialist picture of the world is the failure to understand *how* humans contribute to the world we experience. When science can remove itself from its purely materialistic paradigm and begin to consider phenomena from a different perspective, it will experience a tremendous source of power for new discovery and help for humanity and the planet. Science must have a new theory of knowledge. It needs to develop a theory of the qualities. And to do so, one must start with the qualities and the human mind that experiences these qualities. Let me introduce this approach to you.

The "Inside" of a Wooden Table

Imagine you are sitting at a table made of wood. What we experience as a wooden table has more to it than merely the subatomic particles that seemingly populate it. Our minds, using our senses, also create the table. Our minds are the "inside" of what we experience on the outside as an object. Only in recent decades has quantum science recognized this fact. And our society as a whole does not begin to understand it. As a society we focus on the outside "thing" without realizing that we provide the inside. This entire book aims to make this idea clear, showing how we got here, why it is so hard to understand this, and how we can move beyond it. As a society we have spent so much of our time, energy, and money studying the outside of our world, without recognizing that we have an entire inside that must be illuminated and understood. Our world needs the conscious combination of both to survive.

Here is a way to help you start to think about it: If we had only organs of perception (our five senses) but had done no thinking, the world would be a "blooming, buzzing confusion,"[13] a chaotic environment in which there would be no way to organize or make sense of the innumerable sounds, smells, and sights. This assertion is supported by case studies of blind people who underwent operations to restore their sight at an advanced age but who nevertheless had significant

13   James, *The Principles of Psychology*, p. 462.

difficulty with perceiving the world. Richard L. Gregory's research presented evidence of the high incidence of depression among those whose sight was restored and the high level of difficulty each has in using the new vision. In Gregory's most classic case, he describes the newly sighted man as having little useful perception. "His story is in some ways tragic. He suffered one of the greatest handicaps, and yet he lived with energy and enthusiasm. When his handicap was seemingly swept away, as by a miracle, he lost his peace and his self-respect."

I have worked with deaf and hard-of-hearing people during much of my adult life. I have known deaf people who had no residual hearing but who nevertheless underwent reconstructive middle-ear surgery to restore their ability to hear. They struggled mightily trying to process this new sensory information. After several months, some were so frustrated that they ceased to hear entirely, apparently a psychosomatically. They described the sound as driving them crazy and threatening to destroy their life. To them, common sounds were unintelligible and chaotic. Those who had some small amount of hearing, or who had heard as a child, often find the new ability to hear after surgery helpful and useful, though none of them is ever capable of hearing and understanding in the way that most of us would classify as "normal."

Deafness and blindness in this sense cannot be "cured" because the individuals did not previously learn the requisite thinking necessary for processing the sensory data. They lacked the same sensory organs used by others to organize the world when they were at a young age, and hence, organized the world differently. Lacking these they develop a different perspective and a different way of thinking.[14]

The Inside of Nature

Something organizes all of our sensory experiences in a way that makes sense to us. What is this something? How is this organization accomplished? Understand that *this organization of sensory data occurs in our minds as we think*. The subatomic particles are outside our minds but the perceivers of the subatomic

---

14 Linderman, *The Deaf Story.*

particles, you and I, are within the thinking world. When we unconsciously apply thought to the perceptions picked up via our senses, we experience the macroscopic world we are so familiar with. This familiar natural world that we so easily believe to be objective and independent in and of itself is, indeed, a product of historically hardened habits of thought of which we are no longer aware. These passive habits of thought become inseparable from the sensory data we pick up, and that is why the wooden table exists. It is as if the organizing interface rushes to meet the sensory data at its point of being perceived.

Unfortunately, most of us in the West are completely unaware of our complicity in producing what we experience. We fail to realize that the objective world we experience is a joint venture between our minds (and our sensory organs) and the subatomic world. In essence, then, the macroscopic world of nature and material objects is the quintessential example of the interpenetration of mind and matter. It was never mind or matter. It has always been mind AND matter.

When you think differently, you perceive differently. Aboriginal peoples do not perceive the same world of nature and objects that Westerners perceive. This is the essence of how the awareness—the consciousness—of people can differ. Education and language serve as the primary shapers of how people think. Thinking, perceiving, education, society, and language have been evolving in ways we can discern and learn from. But before getting to that part of the story, it may help to look at the focus of this chapter from a slightly different perspective.

The Unrepresented

To summarize the scientific discussion above, classic physicists (roughly, those physicists who are pre-quantum theory, from Newton through the early twentieth century) had numerous debates concerning qualities. They generally settled on a handful of primary qualities—extension in space, solidity, figure, and motion—and eliminated qualities such as color, smell, and sound as being beyond the bounds of science to adequately address. Now, with the emergence of quantum physics in the twentieth century, *all* qualities have been eliminated from discussion. No longer are the aforementioned primary ones considered fundamental to our physical universe. Instead, quantum physicists have abandoned the notion that macroscopic nature exists independent of humanity. In the quantum world even the "ultimate particle" is not independent of the observer in terms of its behavior (if not its existence). Today's physical scientists assure us that when they examine any material at a subatomic level what they find behaves sometimes as matter and other times as energy.

Barfield calls the subatomic realm, prior to any interaction with human senses, "the unrepresented." The unrepresented does not have what we would call an appearance until it interacts with our sensory organs. When the unrepresented interacts with our senses it becomes represented; that is, it takes on a form. Before it interacts with us (or other sentient beings) you cannot say it has a defined form.

The unrepresented is the "only thing there" (described by physicists as waves and/or particles) prior to interacting with our senses. What we experience as the familiar everyday world, Barfield describes as our "collective representations."[15] As soon as you or I come in contact with the unrepresented (generally when we wake from sleep) we, in a flash, perceive a world of forms, shapes, and "things." These "things," which include size, color, shape and other qualities, appear to us this way because of the unconscious activity of thinking as it interacts with the unrepresented. The only connection we have, as outside observers, with these unrepresented phenomena is at the flash point of thinking. *Thinking inserts itself into the very texture of the unrepresented.* **We must either accept this as truth or reject the theories of physics as an elaborate delusion.** This is why we are focusing on "how" we think.

Subatomic particles are either:

1. Collectively Represented—Put into some form by human minds
2. Unrepresented—Not experienced by human sense organs or technology; in this dynamic state it (they) has no form

---

15 Barfield, *Saving the Appearances.*

Figure 1 (below) gives a basic sense of the limited view of reality we have constructed through our collective representations. It presents one simple means of understanding how our experience of the world, the Collective Representations, is one subset of how we could view the unrepresented. Were we to think differently, or have different sensory organs, or were our current sensory organs developed with different ranges, our experience of the unrepresented could be considerably different. Quantum physics speaks of a number of dimensions beyond the three dimensions of which we are aware. At this point in our physical evolution most Westerners have not developed the physical senses capable of perceiving these world(s). The current "View of Reality" below is merely one of many possibilities.

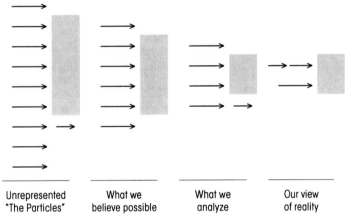

| Unrepresented "The Particles" | What we believe possible | What we analyze | Our view of reality |

Figure 1: "Reality"[16]

16 Adapted from C. Kraft, classroom lecture, School of Intercultural Studies of Fuller Theological Seminary, Pasadena, 1993. I have seemingly equated the particles with the unrepresented in this table. This is a simplification of what I believe to be the case. For Barfield, this was a difficulty he faced, which may be seen in his "Introduction to the Wesleyan Edition" of *Saving the Appearances*. An expanded discussion of this issue would require a lengthy explanation that is beyond the scope of this book.

Concerning "What we analyze" in the diagram above, Steven Quartz of the California Institute of Technology describes how our brains scan our environment and choose what to analyze: "Our brain is computing value at every fraction of a second. Everything that we look at, we form an implicit preference. Some of [our perceptions] make it into our awareness; some of them remain at the level of our unconscious, but [our mind looks]...to find what is of value in our environment."[17] This indicates the power of our attention. Attention is the flashlight of our awareness.

We Must "See" How Our Thinking Interacts with the Unrepresented. Everything we experience has been saturated at all points with thinking. While we cannot "experience" the unrepresented separately from thinking about them, we can conceptually distinguish between them and start our theory of knowledge at that point. We will, therefore, need to abandon the scientific approach of "thinking about" and "knowing about" the world, along with our belief that the truth is some ideal reproduction of some given object. Rather we must recognize that knowledge is contingent on participation in being.[18] We must learn to see that we participate in our world, in what we experience and how we experience it. The kind of knowing we need for our future will be a *knowing from within* ourselves.

Our minds have expectations. The world appears to us in the way we have been conditioned to expect it to appear. It can and does look considerably different to those who have different conditioning. As we interact with people who think differently our collective representations begin to alter. What we "see" will look differently. Perhaps one day we will evolve to reach the point ethno-botanist Terence McKenna termed the "I see what you mean" language.[19] The concept of psycho-social evolution can help in thinking about this.

---

17   Quoted from a column by David Brooks, *New York Times*, Apr. 14, 2009.

18   Barfield, *Romanticism Comes of Age*, p. 252.

19   McKenna and Metzner, 1988 lecture, "Shamanism: Before and beyond

Psycho-social Evolution and Convergence

Biological evolution has taken place over vast periods of time. Considerable research has focused on this type of evolution, building on the seminal work of Charles Darwin. Another type of evolution, the evolution of cultures and civilizations over time, has been receiving scrutiny over the past century by the field of cultural anthropology. This type of evolution, sometimes referred to as psycho-social evolution, involves the self-reproducing and maintaining characteristics of mind, also referred to as "traditions," passed on from generation to generation, and shown by anthropologists to undergo modifications over time.

Not only do societies and civilizations pass on their view of the world through their traditions, ideas themselves evolve. However, unlike biological evolution, ideas evolve in an opposite, convergent way. Variety does not increase as it does in biological evolution, but decreases. One of the characters in a Barfield play states it this way: "I forget how many Bantu languages there are; but I believe it runs into four figures. But as civilization (the name for the latest phase of evolution, the convergent phase) progresses, this variety does not increase."[20] (This contrasts with biological evolution, which produces increasing diversity of species.)

Anthropologists describe the general flow of this convergence in this way. As tribes with complicated polytheisms communicate with other tribes with complicated polytheisms, the polytheisms syncrete with one another, which reduces the total complication. As tribal languages interact and become national instead of merely local, the syncreted polytheisms converge into monotheism. This leads to a further convergence, toward the abstract principle of the uniformity of nature, which underlies all of science. Or, to say it another way, the peoples of the world grow less diverse and more alike as time moves forward. This is not as simple and straightforward as I've

History," http://www.youtube.com/playlist?list=PLE5545AC48EBF0D67.

20 Barfield, *Worlds Apart*, pp. 33–35. This contrasts with biological evolution which produces increasing diversity of species.

indicated—there is more complexity and give-and-take between local and global—but the trend is as stated.

Cultural anthropology has found an important niche in Western academia. It is a move toward the study of evolution from a different angle. However, most anthropologists in the West are, like biologists Green and Depew mentioned earlier, unable to make the leap from a materialistic base to approach these issues from the starting point of the mind, from the "insides."

Summary

In this chapter we have looked at the way Newtonian science was turned on its head by its own methods. Answers to a new way to conceive of the world we live in and experience no longer lie in the direction of further study into the "objects" themselves. Rather, it remains in either of two realms: in mathematical, probabilistic formulae or inside the human mind. In this chapter, I've introduced the concept of the "inside" of objects and it is in that direction we head in the next chapter as we introduce the dynamic of cognition by looking at the evolution of human consciousness.

Chapter 3

THE EVOLUTION OF CONSCIOUSNESS

"A viable and convincing picture of an evolving self-conscious-ness is strangled at birth by the axiom… of belief in a world of subjectless objects."

—OWEN BARFIELD[1]

How humans think and of what humans are aware evolves over time in an interconnected way like an ever-deepening plot and character development in a great novel. We begin our journey into the New Enlightenment with a look at the landscape of Western human history. To help us start, let's take a listen to the thoughts of a hardware store owner, Larry Marshall.

What Do You Think about When You're Alone?

Larry is sitting in a doctor's office waiting for an appointment. The following is a smattering of the thoughts running through his head.

The medical assistant who just came from the patient area and called "Donna" is not happy. I wonder why she doesn't work on that; it's not a good representation for this office. I like the décor here. That guy over there isn't dressed well for the doctor's office; holes in his jeans and he must be 45; should know better. I'm warm, the temp must be near 80 in here. That poor woman must have breathing problems, having to bring an O2 tank around. Nice of them to make coffee for the patients. My neck is stiff, probably from digging up the buckthorn out back

---

1   Barfield, "Self and Reality," in *The Rediscovery of Meaning and Other Essays*, p. 192.

40

yesterday; amazing how that plant grows. Linda and I have a lot left to do on our land. I wonder how Jimmy will do in the Little League game today. He sure has struggled with his arm this year. I hope he's not bored this summer. The drug representative that just walked out from the patient area was dressed to the hilt. I know he's a drug rep because I know that's what they all dress like. I've seen them previous times at physicians' offices since I sometime work with physicians in my work. Also, my friend is a drug rep and has told me a lot about what his work is like and why they have to dress that way. The woman behind the counter looks like a recent Eastern European immigrant; she's attractive, but doesn't use much facial expression… so many doctors' office workers are Eastern European, and now even more and more doctors [and on and on it goes].

The inner chatter that you and I are used to hearing often seems like many overlapping analog radio frequencies, as if we had an ADHD DJ[2] in our head who jumps from station to station. We ponder our preferences—occasionally re-creating some moment of personal pleasure or longing for an imagined future event. We hope for a future filled with health and happiness, dreaming of family, career success, exotic travels, and our own philanthropic role.

Isn't it interesting that not only do you have all these thoughts running through your mind, but you are able to stand outside of them and observe them? When you observe them you become an object of observation within yourself. This ability to stand outside of yourself and observe yourself thinking points to an "observing you" outside of your thoughts.

Notice how we observe and draw conclusions about ourselves through the statements we tell ourselves: "I am outgoing and friendly, full of curiosity, and a pursuer of adventure." Or: "I am intelligent and reserved; I prefer to withhold judgment about people. I take a long time to trust someone enough to share my inner thoughts." These observations and thoughts are all part of our inner life. However, the inner life we take for granted has not always been a part

---

2   Attention Deficit Hyperactivity Disorder Disc Jockey.

of human experience. Had you been born in what we now refer to as the British Isles in AD 243, for example, you would not have had these types of inner thoughts. Nor would you view yourself as witty or outgoing, studious or charming. You would not conceptualize your life with these individualistic terms. **You would not have an inner life at all. No one did.**

Human inner life developed and evolved over the course of millennia. This development of inner life is a core result of the evolution of consciousness. Inner life reached its fullness with the spreading of the logical thought that resulted from the Enlightenment. The quality of consciousness for a human being, or that of which individuals are aware, has evolved through time. We have awareness that non-Enlightenment humans did not have. Those humans who are pre-logical have awareness that we do not have. This assertion will be demonstrated in the coming pages and shown to be central to an understanding of New Enlightenment thinking.

In his research into pre-Enlightenment literature (literature written prior to the sixteenth century), Barfield demonstrates how one can trace this evolution of human inner life by observing changes in the use of language. These changes, in word formation and use, indicate a gradual increase in awareness of the self as a separate individual. With the advent of the Enlightenment, this increase in both awareness of *self*-consciousness and the increase of rational thought (which includes increased abstraction and use of logic) move in parallel. Immanuel Kant, Barfield tells us, demonstrated this point quite effectively when he showed how self-consciousness could not have existed prior to logical thought.[3]

To those who may suggest that human beings did have a rich inner life prior to the Enlightenment but had yet to discover it, Barfield replies:

> Some "discoveries" take place because they haven't been seen yet; others take place because they were not and now are, they come to be. The "discovery" of the inner world was a discovery

---

3   Barfield, *Poetic Diction: A Study in Meaning*, p. 208.

of something that did not exist. It simply does not make sense to say that at one time self-consciousness was an existing fact that had not yet been discovered. You cannot be unaware of being aware.[4]

An Overview of the Evolution of Consciousness

I noted earlier that the evolution of consciousness, as it relates to the development of the human as a self-conscious individual, is an evolution from consciousness that was originally un-individuated. In other words, consciousness existed, but it rested in the collective rather than the individual. Its evolution can be seen by a panorama of history. In the following sections of this overview, we will take some broad introductory sweeps across history, showing in particular the evolution of consciousness typical in the West. You will become acquainted with how the thought of the time period, as evidenced in the words and writings of the time, demonstrate changes in human consciousness. You will also note that I present this evolution not from the perspective of so much of modern science, which views consciousness as evolving from irrational matter. Rather, I present it as evolving from collectivity to individuality.

From World Consciousness to Ancient Greece

Historians tell us that the earth's first great civilization, ancient Egypt, consisted of a unified theocratic power that ruled society. What we today would call basic human labor rights did not exist. A group of individual humans were not considered individuals— they constituted a collective. Evidence from the writings of their time is minimal, but what remains, generally in forms of myths and epics, reveals a consciousness that can be described as world-consciousness. Thinking involved pictures and figures which came to them much as well-formed ideas come to us in our minds. This is the type of consciousness where humans "participated"

---

4   Barfield, "Philology and the Incarnation," in *The Rediscovery of Meaning and Other Essays*, pp. 267–268 (emphasis added).

fully; that is, individuals did not see or feel themselves as something other, or separate from the world around them, but viewed themselves as a part of the all-encompassing "river of life," flowing in tandem with nature. Nature came to them alive, and their experience within her compares to our experience of the flow of thoughts within our inner life.

The ancient Egyptians focused outside of their self. Their consciousness did not include self-consciousness. A simple but useful comparison would be to imagine humanity as a hand, and the rest of existence as the whole body. Similar to how a hand works in tandem with the body and would not consider its "rights" or its individuality, so, too, did the individuals of that time period feel as if they were a part of the world without self-rights, self-determination, or even the ability to grasp those concepts. This does not mean that they did not know they were individuals with names and some sort of identity. They had individual names but their focus went outward, rather than inside themselves. Their identity centered in their connection with the collective.

With the development of Mesopotamian and, especially ancient Greek civilization, language evolved from primarily oral to a mixture of oral and written. We have ample writings, including philosophical, poetic/epic, and what can be described as parochial history, from which to develop an understanding of their worldview. One feature of ancient literature concerns the universality all cultures had of describing a fall from a paradise or Golden Age.[5] One cannot help but wonder why no ancient myth described or at least hinted at a human evolution from animals.

The ancient Greek language was verb dominated and nature related. Barfield points out numerous examples that help clarify the difference in how the Greeks saw the world. For the ancient Greek, the idea of static nouns did not exist. One did not think of a man, for example, as having a beard, either in the sense of possessing one, nor in the sense of the beard as a motionless "thing." Rather,

---

5   Barfield, *Worlds Apart: A Dialogue of the 1960s*, pp. 158–159.

the Greek word gives the sense of activity and movement, which would be more accurately translated as "bearding is happening." As another example, Greeks did not think of someone as young in the sense of possessing youth, but rather their term is akin to the active verb "flowering."

All nouns invoked a living, changing sense. Our use of nouns, on the other hand, focuses on the finished product; an after-the-fact view that, in essence, looks at everything in the past tense. "He has a beard" makes a statement about a finished product, while "bearding is happening" gives the sense of one being in the middle of a process. It is true that we may say, "He is growing a beard" but, by definition, the Greeks said that every time they said the word "beard,"[6] regardless of whether the beard was "finished" or not.

Concerning an individual's view of oneself, Barfield notes that there is little, if any, evidence that the Greeks were moved by the beauty of nature, or, more precisely, little evidence that they were ever moved in such a way as to be aware of themselves as moved by it; in other words, the evidence reveals little (if any) inner life.[7] Barfield, quoting Samuel Taylor Coleridge, points out that there are few adverbs in Homer's epic the *Iliad:*

> With more adverbs there would have been some subjectivity, or subjectivity would have made them. The Greeks were just then on the verge of the bursting forth of individuality.[8]

Similarly, psychologist and noted Princeton lecturer Julian Jaynes notes how, in the *Iliad* for example, no one spent time trying to figure out what to do in a given situation or how they could control the outcome of a particular circumstance. Instead, each character is constantly being pushed and pulled by the gods. One conceived of one's self as part of the larger whole of humanity. Those who ruled were chosen by the gods as rulers. In the *Iliad,* "it is the gods

---

6   Barfield, *Romanticism Comes of Age*, pp. 51–58.
7   Ibid., p. 233.
8   Barfield, *What Coleridge Thought*, p. 162.

who start quarrels among men that really cause the war, and then plan its strategy."[9]

In the *Odyssey*, assumed by most scholars to have been written much later than the *Iliad*, Jaynes notes the first evidence of the beginning of individual consciousness. In the *Odyssey* Odysseus deceives Athene, an act of will unthinkable in the *Iliad*. Jaynes emphasizes that the space in which this choice is made has moved from an outer realm to a realm of Odysseus's mind. Much of the outer control of the gods remains, but the age of the complete domination by the gods has begun its many-centuries evolution toward individuality.

Many classics scholars assume that the Greek writers' descriptions of the gods controlling human affairs are examples of "poetic license." For this to be true assumes that the people of that era thought the way we think and that their writers were simply "metaphorizing" the gods. No evidence exists to make this assumption. We do not find this type of use of metaphor in any literature of this time. Scholars often fail to realize that when the myths came into being, our current taken-for-granted distinction between the subjective and objective did not and could not have existed. As noted above, subjectivity and self-consciousness are inseparable from rational or discursive thought operating in abstract ideas, a type of thinking that did not begin to predominate in language and education until the dawn of the Enlightenment more than twenty centuries later. We have to look elsewhere for an understanding of the ancient Greeks' use of language.

From Aristotle to the Enlightenment

The first recorded "thinking about thinking," or reflective thinking, came courtesy of Aristotle in the fourth century BCE. He proposed a separation between the senses and the mind and introduced the beginnings of an inductive method. He remained fundamentally pantheistic—that is, all of nature and humanity are connected to, and part of, the "The Logos," understood by most to mean God,

---

9   Jaynes, *The Origin of Consciousness in the Breakdown of the Bicameral Mind.*

Source and/or universal Mind. His observation of his own thinking process can be said to be the first evidence in recorded history of one who did not view the world as exclusively comprised of external circumstances (i.e. that all human activity is besieged and controlled by the whims of the gods).

However, not until the writing of the Stoics during the first centuries AD did anyone explicitly articulate a *division* between self on the one side and environment on the other. With this division, the move toward the "self" as a center began. While the actual emergence of the "self," with individual rights and the encouragement to pursue "life, liberty, and happiness," would take many centuries to be realized, the first flickers of genuine self-consciousness emerged during this time. In a little over a millennium, Western humanity would begin to define itself by its individuality, not its collectivity. It would also see itself as separated from nature, the earth, and the cosmos, rather than flowing and in harmony with them. This division also nudged humanity toward the gradual development of an internal, immaterial language, one that enabled an inner world, exemplified by our hardware store owner Larry, to emerge within individuals.

Within medieval society, evolution of consciousness proceeded slowly. Western society continued to identify as a collective society as well as a society in harmony with nature. One way to illustrate the sense of life for a medievalist comes from physicist Roger Jones, who provides a picture of how the medievalist experienced space (both earth's atmosphere [air] and outer space). Space for the medievalist was not primarily about distance or emptiness but about relationship:

> The space of medieval consciousness...is organic, connec-
> tive, nurturing, human, intelligent, alive with meaning. It is a
> realm of wisdom and a storehouse of knowledge. Rather than
> space, it is place, home, and environment. Like a womb to an
> embryo, it sustains, warms, and nurtures; it provides balms
> and lifeline: it has no clear-cut boundaries, no separation

between inner and outer. Although less sharply defined, clean, and geometrical than our space, it contains things that we would not think of as spatial at all, things psychological, emotional, and intuitive. One's feeling for others and for other living and inanimate things are included, so that the sense of medieval space incorporates love, appreciation, inspiration, belonging, kinship, and holiness.

Jones contrasts our current sense of space with the medieval sense:

In modern times, our lost sense of synthesis or connection has become intellectualized as an assumption about reality (that it is separate and independent of our inner mental world and, in fact, subsumes that inner world, which is therefore not real). We conceive of space as infinity, empty, lifeless, cold, dark, alien, void. It is the blank, unfeeling stage on which matter plays out its aimless, random acts. It provides the merest, tiniest corner in which to harbor an insignificant speck of a planet, warmed by a second-rate star, on which by sheer accident, against impossible odds, life and finally consciousness have come to be. We see ourselves as living in a basically alien universe which offers us little succor or hope, and above all, no meaning or purpose.

Our modern space is the perfect metaphor for separation, extension, individuation, and alienation. We cannot even conceive of existence except in space, which then become the medium par excellence of existence.... Space is the background from which we emerge and exist. On the one side of the coin is existence and uniqueness, on the other, alienation and isolation. Our spatial metaphor is thus intimately linked with our fears and apprehensions about life, death and survival.[10]

In the medieval world one felt much more a vital part of things. One *belonged* to the earth and the universe. As Jones describes, this "home" constituted a great organism within which human individuals functioned meaningfully and purposefully. People felt

10 Jones, *Physics as Metaphor.*

and sensed meaning and purpose. The stars in the sky and the minerals of the earth were not separated from humans by space. They were connected to people as if through invisible energy or umbilical cords. Vast distances were not even conceived. One felt at home, supported, and succored. Life might at times be difficult, but never foreign, disjointed, or isolated. Death and pain might be frightening, but not annihilating.

During the later Middle Ages, the Crusades, which occurred during the twelfth and thirteenth centuries, resulted in an unexpected push of the West toward Enlightenment. Designed primarily as a means of recapturing territory from the Jews and Muslims believed to belong to the Christian West, the Crusades resulted in interaction between Scholastics in the European universities with the more advanced Islamic scholars. The Scholastics began incorporating Islamic deductive logic with their studies of Aristotelian logic, further moving the West closer to Enlightenment thinking.

Another milestone occurred in England during the thirteenth century, as belief in the divine right of kings began to be questioned, resulting eventually in the issuance of The Magna Carta in 1215. This declaration by the King of England introduced the right for citizens to be judged by their peers in a court of law. This marked a major advancement of individual human rights, which eventually led to Western societies operating according to common and constitutional law.

Another clear sign of the emergence of inner life can be seen by the emergence of the concept of "conscience." Its use in pre-Medieval times in the Latin language connoted a shared quality that no individual possessed; a communal force in which each individual partook. During the late medieval period the word and its associated meaning changed to refer to a semi-personified and private mentor—i.e., a similar meaning as the word carries today.[11]

---

11 Barfield, *History in English Words*, p. 133.

Beginning of the Enlightenment in Western Civilization

As the Renaissance began to flower in sixteenth century Europe, new approaches to the arts and sciences emerged and proliferated. Events and inventions changed the perspective of Western humanity. Chief among the inventions was the printing press, which allowed writings to be copied. Philosophers' writings began to be read widely, resulting in long-distance interactions between intellectual leaders. This also accelerated the speed at which new thoughts arose, were discussed, and became enhanced. The proliferation of imaginative thinking that resulted produced the work of Galileo, Newton, and Bacon, among others.

With the increase of interaction among leading thinkers, the very consciousness of individuals changed. As interior thought increased and philosophers realized what was occurring within them, various writers attempted to explain the dramatic changes humanity was undergoing. No one explained it as succinctly and clearly as Descartes and his famous axiom (1643), "I think, therefore I know I am." With the separation of mind, which Descartes believed to be the only certainty one could not doubt, he proceeded to propagate the method of analysis we Enlightenment thinkers know so well: the division of all problems and ideas into their smallest units and arranging them in their most logical order.

With this Cartesian[12] division between mind and matter, Descartes formulated "the insulation of matter from mind as a philosophical principle." He wrote:

> The methodology of natural science is erected on that principle. It was by the rigorous exclusion from its field, under the name of "occult qualities," of every element, whether spiritual or mental or called by any other name, which can only be conceived as non-material, and therefore non-measurable, that natural knowledge acquired a precision unknown before the revolution—because inherently impossible in terms of the old fusion; and, armed with that precision (entitling it to the

---

12   *Cartesian* refers to the thought of Descartes.

name of "science"), went on to achieve its formidable techno-logical victories.[13]

Most leading thinkers of the time adhered to this division of mind from matter, which led to great advancements in the study of matter. Combined with the scientific method, first fully articulated by the late sixteenth century by Francis Bacon, philosophers and newly emerging scientists were able to propose the inductive method. By focusing on the data collected via human senses, this method became the alternative to the deductive method of the Scholastics of the pre-Enlightenment.[14] This new "scientific method" required individuals to conceive of themselves as separate from what they studied. Consequently, scientists could act as detached subjects—observers, investigators, and analyzers—in a world filled with objects: hence the Cartesian subject/object divide.

Bacon's scientific method and the Cartesian divide led directly to the development of Enlightenment thinking characterized by "The Belief." Over the following four centuries this type of thinking has come to dominate the thinking of most Westerners. Little of the former, synthetic way of thinking has remained in Western societies. Enlightenment thinking now controls our education system and is virtually unchallenged by any other system of thought. It has so permeated our language that it is difficult to conceive how to think differently.

Bacon and his contemporaries created numerous words during the sixteenth century that signify the subject/object way of thinking. Such new words as discovery, skeptical, experiment, crucial, instance, curiosity, inquisitive, analyze, distinguish, inspect, ancient, modern, progressive, scrutinize, and investigate show the emerging scientific mindset of the Enlightenment era. These words provided anchoring points to fledgling scientific thinking. One could, for

---

13 Barfield, "Introduction," in Steiner, *The Case for Anthroposophy*.

14 Deductive reasoning, which flourished during the high Middle Ages among the Scholastics, involves an argument that shows a conclusion flows naturally from a set of premises. The Scholastics used this method primarily with their study of the Bible.

example, use one's *curiosity* in order to *investigate* and *experiment* with "objective" forces of nature such as water and steam power. These words did not exist prior to the sixteenth century.

Also, a sense of development and progress emerged early in the seventeenth century. Barfield's research of all pre-seventeenth-century dictionaries—Greek, Latin, English—show no sense of the "march of history." In the pre-seventeenth century world, "history" consisted of cycles and recurring series of events rather than any sort of progression.

It may be difficult to imagine, but those of the Middle Ages were not trying to progress, evolve, or find new and improved ways of living. Rather, they were trying to "regenerate" or "amend" and become more in harmony with what they understood to be the "first" man or woman, a desire to return to the garden of Eden and the innocence of the Adam figure.[15]

Internalization and New Words. Without the subject/object divide, humans could not have evolved to the point where the concept of a "me" could crystallize. We are so accustomed to operating as a human from "within," we do not realize that the objective/subjective dualism is not fundamental to how humans used to experience the world. One learns to extract one's individuality in Western societies during early childhood. Psychologist James Baldwin describes the way all of us as children drew our subjectivity out of perception and thought: "[The child] achieves the wonderful step whereby all objects alike become *his* objects, *his* content of meaning, *his* experience."[16] Our Western orientation toward children, from the way we speak to them to the way we explain the world of objects around them, leads them to this "discovery" of their individuality.

In an Enlightenment world, we view ourselves as separate from other individuals, with considerable choice concerning the types of thoughts and ideas we contemplate. Though this book does not debate the issue of individual free will, the whole concept of

---

15   Barfield, *History in English Words*, pp. 167–168.

16   Quoted by Barfield, *Poetic Diction*, p. 205.

individual freedom, and the general belief in it, pervades Western thinking. This was never true at any point in human history prior to the Enlightenment. To repeat from the previous chapter, "It simply does not make sense to say that at one time self-consciousness was an existing fact that had not yet been discovered. You cannot be unaware of being aware."[17] This is why the *Iliad* does not contain instances where individuals purposefully chose certain actions. Internal freedom, and awareness of free will, comes from awareness of the self as an individual, which, for Western humanity, evolved and became strong through rational thought and the subject/object divide of the Enlightenment.

The emergence of widespread internal thought and individuation occurred in conjunction with the sixteenth-century Protestant Reformation. Prior to this time, Church leaders held The Inquisition to root out thoughts determined to be incongruent with orthodox Christian beliefs. In *The Brothers Karamazov*, Dostoevsky conveys a sense of the Medieval Church's perspective: Jesus is said to return to a European Medieval village and begins to heal people and speak to them of their free choice. He is again sentenced to death, this time by the church. The church Archbishop explains to Jesus that people cannot yet to be trusted to handle free thought. Dostoevsky's parable illustrates that the time for internalization of thought had not yet arrived. It also points to the role served by the medieval church to prevent humanity from moving further away from the age of Paradise, prior to the "Fall" from grace into sin. With the coming of the Reformation, the Church moved from its exclusive focus on external observances and rituals that require the mediation of a priest toward an emphasis on the centrality of the individual and the "inwardness of all true grace."[18]

History in English Words. Barfield's *History in English Words* surveys the evolution toward individualization of consciousness by

---

17   Barfield, "Self and Reality," in *The Rediscovery of Meaning and Other Essays*,
       pp. 266–267.

18   Barfield, *History in English Words*, p. 158.

extensively reviewing the different occasions and circumstances that resulted in the creation of words (or changes to existing words) in the English language. My brief summary in this section provides a small sample of his remarkable presentation.

During the sixteenth and seventeenth centuries, new words were formed that showed the move toward individualistic centrality. Hyphenated words in particular demonstrate this shift (i.e., self-love, self-confidence, self-knowledge, and self-esteem, among others). Many existing words took on clear shifts of meaning—conscience, disposition, spirit, temper, gentle, perceive, religion, happy, sad, and sin. Each had previously been used to indicate an external generation (from the gods or the environment), rather than our current usage of each to describe a point of generation from within an individual.

At the same time, many words previously used to describe the outer world began to be viewed as describing the inside of the person—depression, emotion, embarrassment, agitation, apathy, homesickness, disappointment, and excitement are some examples. Also, an entirely new class of words developed that described the effects external things have on individuals—amusing, boring, charming, entertaining, exciting, fascinating, interesting, and pathetic.

At no time prior to the seventeenth century were these words used in a way that denote an inner experience.[19] For example, consider two friends describing the M. Night Shyamalan movie "Sixth Sense." One says, "The movie was so interesting. I was charmed by the young boy and found the entire experience very entertaining." Another says, "I was bored. Nothing excited me. The use of trickery at the end was pathetic." Would you say the movie was interesting or not? Of course, the answer is that it depends. It depends on the interior view of the individual. The movie itself cannot *be* any of the words used to describe each friend's reaction, since they were describing their internal perspective. That is, the movie is "exciting" *only if* an individual expresses his or her own opinion about it.

---

19   This is central to Barfield's *History in English Words.*

Although a movie may contain features consistent with other movies that may be described as "exciting," those features do not make the movie "exciting" within itself. Individuals simply did not use words in this way prior to this time in history nor would they likely have been able to talk about their own reaction to seeing one.

Changes in Literary Forms. Literary forms also evolved through these time periods. A simple version of literary form evolution would be as follows:

Sagas	Myths	Epics	Prophetic	Philosophical Treatises	Letters		Essays	Memoirs	Novels/History

2700		1000		500		0	1000	1500		1900

Often scholars will classify early writings—sagas, myths, epics—as poetry, given that they were sound-based. The modern "essay" is usually dated as having begun with Michel Montaigne, in the late 1600s, and the first "novels" are usually considered to be epistolary ones written in the 1700s, with the non-epistolary novel form exploding in the nineteenth century.

Obviously, these are broad classifications. There are currently hundreds of sub-classifications of each literary genre, each with its own history. [20] But such microanalysis is unnecessary to point out the fact that literary forms have clearly evolved over time. The development of prose texts co-evolved with more and more "separation" between perceiver and perceived, our subject/object divide. Shakespeare provides the first example of the repeated use of soliloquy. Consider Hamlet's "To be or not to be." He speaks from within his own considerations and his own self-protection. Should he trust or not, and how does he "feel" about that? Such internalization did not occur previously since humanity had yet to evolve such an inner life.

---

20   This taxonomy of literary forms and discussion that follows draws from the work of J. Nichols, associate professor, Utah Valley University Department of English and Literature, personal correspondence, Dec. 3, 2010.

Quite recently, a new literary form has emerged called creative nonfiction. As a new form, creative nonfiction moves literature to the place where subject and object are no longer separate, and "outer" and "inner" perceptions are more and more consciously integrated. This parallels the type of evolution described in the story of Sekem and what the New Enlightenment way of thinking strives to achieve. A number of well-known twentieth century classics, including George Orwell's *Down and out in Paris and London*, James Baldwin's *Notes of a Native Son*, Ernest Hemingway's *Death in the Afternoon*, and Tom Wolfe's *The Right Stuff*, were written with this style. As a key website for the promotion of this genre describes:

> Creative nonfiction... not only allows but also encourages the writer to become a part of the story or essay being written. The personal involvement creates a special magic that alleviates the suffering and anxiety of the writing experience; it provides many outlets for satisfaction and self-discovery, flexibility and freedom.[21]

Increasing interdependence. Ironically, this evolution to inner-individualization has made us *more* interdependent. During nineteenth century industrialization, individuals no longer produced within localized communities; larger societies with people depending on one another became the norm. New technology transformed the way people worked. Economic life was freed from the legal and religious domains through the development and propagation of a free-market economic system. Many governmental and religious controls on capital were discarded. Industrialization spread with new technology and systematic division of labor became widespread. This resulted in new relationships within Western societies whereby the production of goods and services became highly interdependent.

---

21   At http://www.creativenonfiction.org/thejournal/whatiscnf.htm.

In essence, we have become more interdependent than at any point in our history. My favorite ink pen, a sac filler pen, is quite a modern marvel. It is constructed of several raw materials, some of which are mined, others created chemically in a laboratory, and others created in factories. Numerous, perhaps countless, people had a hand in creating my pen. From the workers in the companies who made the machinery, to those who removed it from the ground, to those who delivered the material to the assembly factory, to those who handle accounting and quality, to the parents and teachers who educated each of these workers, to those who provided a stable society for the commerce, and on and on. We are interdependent across societies and nations in ways never seen before on this earth, even as we have become more internally individualized.

Change in View of Psychology. Another recent change concerns how we view ourselves and our psyches. At the beginning of the twentieth century, during the height of Enlightenment thinking within higher education, Sigmund Freud and C. G. Jung introduced new concepts by focusing on thought and its internal psychological influences. Prior to the twentieth century there was little if any awareness of an "unconscious" element in humanity, and by the time Freud and Jung died, the "common person" was speaking about the unconscious—an amazingly quick change of perspective. Jung notes this lack of awareness in a letter to J. B. Rhine dated July 26, 1954, where he said, "Certain main points of my book (*Synchronicity: An Acausal Connecting Principle*[22]) have not been understood at all, but that is what I have always seen with my books: I just have to wait for about ten or twenty years until certain readers appear understanding what my thought is."[23]

---

22 Jung, *Synchronicity*.

23 Mansfield et al., "The Rhine–Jung Letters: Distinguishing Parapsychological from Synchronistic Events" (*The Journal of Parapsychology*: 1998: vol. 62:2–25).

Overlaps between the Time Periods. There are natural overlaps between the time periods described above. Even today many rural people of developing countries fit more into a non-Enlightenment mentality than in any of the others, though the numbers of these groups shrink annually through the dramatic increase in cross-cultural interaction and communication via new communication technologies.

Inner Language and Outer Language. The changes in language discussed in the sections above indicate the remarkable transformations that have led to contemporary Western consciousness. New words, new ideas, and a new way to think have become part of our ingrained habits of mental life, as well as a growing and rich interior life that has been evolving for centuries.

At the same time, Enlightenment thinking and the scientism born of "The Belief" produced new metaphors to describe the study of the exteriors of nature and matter. Chief among these metaphors is that of the machine with its corresponding term, mechanics. This metaphor led to the view that even living organisms can be broken down to their core "material," which would allow us to unlock the mystery of how organisms "work." This belief became the basis of biology and Western medicine. Previous knowledge of a consciousness that included a strong connection to nature waned to the point that today our society does not value that type of pre-Enlightenment wisdom and knowledge. We have evolved to an era of strong individuality with a rich inner language, but we also have a dominant paradigm, that of scientism.

Western societies do not even seem aware that there is a strong tension between the fact of our rich interior lives and the theory of knowledge of "The Belief," which considers only the outside. Nor do we seem aware of the strong limitations of "The Belief" to explain living systems. This despite the proclamation of National Medal of Science winner Paul Alfred Weiss, who laments that with all of the successes in applying analytic methods to the study of living organisms, analysis "can yield no complete explanation of the behavior of even the most elementary living system."[24] Likely one difficulty involves our perspective on Charles Darwin's theory of evolution.

A Perspective on Darwinian Evolution

Did we evolve from a mindless universe? Can a mindless, irrational universe produce mind? Darwinism teaches that genetic variation is a chance occurrence, and that the environment determines which variations are selected and passed on as traits in a population. In essence, mutations arise randomly in the DNA and the resulting variations with hardiness survive. Given vast amounts of time, the process of natural selection results in the evolution of ever-more complex organisms. I do not wish to challenge Darwinian theory. His way of describing the evolution of matter that accounts for the variation of species and the diversity of naturally occurring phenomena is an elegant and powerful theory.

We must, however, understand the limitations of Darwin's theory. Darwin produced *On the Origin of Species by Means of Natural Selection* at a period of history when *self*-consciousness had so fully achieved its ascendancy that humans could no longer feel any extrasensory link with natural phenomena in participation; hence one could not even conceptualize a prehistory wherein matter and mind were not separate but interpenetrated. In other words, Darwin wrote his most influential works during the Enlightenment period. Regardless of what he personally thought concerning "mind" and human consciousness, his research focused on the evolution of matter. Readers of Darwin, unconsciously steeped in "The Belief," draw the conclusion that mind evolved from irrational, amoral matter. This conclusion fails to realize the limits of the Enlightenment framework within which Darwin operated.

Had he looked at the history of the world from the point of view of the evolution of consciousness, he would likely have developed a complementary theory to the one I am in the process of unfolding in this book. For those who take the time to understand the

---

24   Weiss, *The Science of Life*, p. 267.

evolution of consciousness, it will be as if you begin to see what it looks like to view objects three-dimensionally when they had previously only been flat. Understanding the evolution of consciousness does not discount Darwin's work—it enhances it by altering how we view nature.

Physical science has a difficult time with this concept. Evolutionary biologists wish to explain everything from a material base. But consciousness is not physiological, and the way to understand it requires a different analysis as there are no bones to compare. The evolution of consciousness can "only" be phenomenological, which by definition requires that our focus be on the analysis of inner experiences.

Summary

By looking at the historical framework of the evolution of consciousness, we have covered a central principle necessary to understand the theory of knowledge of the New Enlightenment. We saw how human consciousness, during the era since the Enlightenment, has included an increase in inner language along with an increase of nouns due to the creation of the subject/object divide. Our sense of our own individuality and the primacy this has taken in our views of the world evolved simultaneously with the subject/object divide.

Human recognition of the unconscious emerged with the work of Sigmund Freud and C. G. Jung. At the same time, participation with the world decreased during the Enlightenment era to the point where most Westerners had no awareness of how their minds participated with the phenomena to produce the macroscopic world. Instead of being involved synthetically (in sync) with the ebb and flow of existence, we see ourselves as detached observers of a world going on by itself. While this has led to significant advances in technology and medicine, it is insufficient for us to take the next evolutionary step.

We must recognize that sense impressions do not happen to us passively. Rather, we participate in the creation of the "thing" we experience, such as a wooden table, as discussed in chapter 2. As Barfield states, "We must have intimate acquaintance with customary processes of our own intellects and apply real effort of the imagination."[25] Beginning in the next chapter we will look more deeply into the way our minds create meaning and participate in the appearance of the world we experience around us.

---

25 Barfield, *Romanticism Comes of Age*, p. 50.

Chapter 4

HOW DO WE KNOW ANYTHING:
THE ACTIVITY OF THINKING

"We see the world in terms of our theories"
—Thomas Kuhn
(*The Structures of Scientific Revolution*)

Ask yourself two related questions: How can you take seriously the dramatic gulf between what science says makes up the universe (tiny subatomic particles/waves of some sort, made up of 99.99% empty space) and your experiences of the familiar world (with its objects made up of surfaces, smells, tastes, weight, and size, such as rocks, waterfalls, rainbows, automobiles, or daffodils)? And, why are physicists telling us that an electron isn't there until we look for it, or that it can be in two places at once, since this is so contrary to the logic of "The Belief" as it is drawn from classic Newtonian physics?

Take your answers and now ask yourself, "How do I know what I know: On what do I base my knowledge?" "The Belief" does not help solve these quantum riddles that baffle our minds. It seems impossible to believe that solid objects are mostly made up of empty space. We have yet to develop a common way of thinking, a common language, that can handle the paradoxes that physicists have uncovered in our world. Consequently, we continue living each day thinking in a way based on the science of the nineteenth century. What will it take to change our common, everyday way of thinking into thinking fit for the twenty-first century?

Thinking

Often philosophers discuss topics without talking about what it means to "know and think." They speak about the ego, the mind, brain functions, nature, life, or even consciousness, but fail to acknowledge that they are discussing something already formed, something on which "cognitive activity has already been expended."[1] These words have weight and convey meaning.

How did your thoughts about these words get there in the first place? If you take a moment to ponder this, you may respond that somehow these thoughts enter you mind through the process of creating meaning that comes from learning to understand and use language. You surmise that children pick up this ability to think these thoughts through some sort of a building way; i.e., block upon block, precept upon precept.

While this has some truth it still fails to realize that the use of language requires an ability to think. The first possible move we can make toward knowing anything is through "thinking." Thinking occurs prior to any activity or conceptualization or language. This focus on the thinking process is part of a discipline known in philosophical circles as epistemology, the study of our "knowing." To say it another way, it is the study of the inner dynamic of our cognitive abilities.

In order to craft a new theory of knowledge we must start with thinking and learn how it happens. This chapter and the following chapters will unfold how we think and will suggest an answer to the question, "Where can science find new impetus, given that its current models are limited in their understanding of the nature of reality?" As discussed in chapter 2, the direction of twenty-first century science is away from classical physics and toward an approach that incorporates the findings of quantum physics. At the same time there is a sense of uncertainty, both within science and within Western societies, regarding the new understandings that are yet to emerge to the consciousness of society. Having given

---

1   Barfield, *Romanticism Comes of Age*, p. 244.

up the premises of classic science, what are new premises for an expanded science?

Only when we create a common language to talk about our mind will we be able to forge new premises. These new premises must have the ability to investigate the qualities of our world that science has deemed outside the realm of scientific investigation (i.e., anything that can be influenced by the human mind such as color, smell, shape, or feel). Any **new** methods for investigating the phenomena of our world should combine the scientific/traditional method with one that understands how the human mind works. This combination will look both to the outside of the phenomena and the inside. That is, besides just analyzing the outside of a table—important in its own right—we must examine the inside—how our minds participated in getting the table there in the first place. We have a long way to go to accomplish this. We have more than 400 years of classic science's focus on the outside. Western society has only barely begun to look at the inside. To help us talk about this, let's look at the concept of "participation."

Participation

At the end of chapter 2, we looked at subatomic behavior and the collective representations that result when humans interact with the unrepresented. These representations are our experience of the objective world and are formed through our interaction with the unrepresented. Barfield terms this process *participation*. This term effectively communicates that we as people participate with creating the material world we experience. But until we dig into it, our participation is unconscious. That is, the world as it appears has already been formed for us without us recognizing the role of our cognition.

Beginning a New Enlightenment Lexicon

1. Unrepresented—the subatomic particles/waves as they exist prior to human participation

2. Participation—the process where humans, with their sensory organs and their minds, encounter the unrepresented and experience the unrepresented as a form of matter
3. Collective representations—the forms of matter that commonly appear when humans of a particular era participate with the unrepresented
4. Conscious participation—the experience where individuals will be both individually conscious (that is, fully aware of themselves as distinct individuals) and aware of how they, as individuals, are interconnected to the external world of nature in a unified whole

Using this concept of "participation" helps us imagine how pre-Enlightenment humans participated in a way that perceived the world as an interconnected unity, an experience quite different than is experienced by Westerners after the Enlightenment period begins. After the Enlightenment each views one's self as a separate and distinct object among other objects in empty space. In the pictures and thoughts in our minds, we perceive no direct physical/spiritual connections to one another.

Both pre-Enlightenment and Enlightenment experiences in participation are in essence unconscious unless we make the effort to step back and learn what is taking place in participation. The process of stepping back and observing our own participation will allow us to experience a theme that is central to the New Enlightenment, that of conscious participation. In conscious participation, we seek means to regain our sense of connections to the world while maintaining our knowledge of our individuality. There are a number of examples of communities that are currently practicing conscious participation. One of them is the Egyptian community of Sekem.

Sekem

Egypt is known for its high quality cotton, prized by connoisseurs of fine linens the world over. Imagine a cotton farm in Egypt that could produce a higher quality and higher yield of cotton, while simultaneously reducing pesticide use by more than ninety-seven percent. It sounds too good to be true, yet that's exactly what the Egyptian community Sekem has accomplished since 1977. Sekem's exemplary success has resulted from synthesizing non-Enlightenment agriculture with current science.

Sekem, founded in 1977 by Dr. Ibrahim Abouleish, is self-described as an initiative "founded to realize the vision of sustainable human development." The community website's opening page declares:

> Sekem aims to contribute to the comprehensive development of the individual, society and environment. A holistic concept encompassing integrated economic, social and cultural development forms the key Sekem vision. Through his biodynamic agricultural methods, Dr. Abouleish received the Right Livelihood Award [the "Alternative Nobel Prize"] for establishing a business model for the twenty-first century in which commercial success is integrated with and promotes the social and cultural development of society through economics of love.[2]

A Bit of Background. Ibrahim Abouleish, born in Egypt in 1937, moved to Austria to study chemistry and medicine at the age of 19. By the time he returned to live in Egypt in 1977, he was an accomplished pharmacologist, having been granted numerous patents for medicines to treat a number of ailments. He returned to Egypt with a vision for developing part of the Egyptian desert into an economic center for herbal remedies and organic food products, which ultimately resulted in the founding of Sekem. Dr. Abouleish, however, faced significant battles during these times. He not only had to learn government regulations, banking, business, and marketing—more than enough of a challenge for three lifetimes—he was attacked and threatened by some of the world's most well-known multinational chemical companies due to his revolutionary biodynamic agriculture methods (a non-Enlightenment method of

---

2   See http://www.Sekem.com/.

farming explained below) that substantially lessened the need to use such chemicals for cotton farming.

Between 1992 and 1995, Sekem demonstrated to the governmental agriculture minister the efficacy of their biodynamic agricultural process. Convinced that it represented a step forward in farming, the Egyptian government ordered the cessation of pesticide use (35,000 tons were used in 1995) from crop dusting planes. Within a few weeks, multinational chemical companies—upset that their business was plummeting—began accusing members of the Sekem community as sun-worshipers in the large daily papers of Cairo. As Ibrahim Abouleish describes it, "Worshipping the sun for Muslims is like worshipping Satan for Europeans." In this predominantly Muslim country, the accusations threatened the entire Sekem community as well as the decision of the government to cease crop dusting.

To address these threats, Abouleish organized a meeting with the prominent sheiks, government leaders, and imams of Egypt. Over the course of a tension-filled day, Abouleish used the Qur'an to explain Sekem's agricultural methods; by the end of the day, the Egyptian leaders were convinced of the congruence of Sekem with Islam. In fact, when the imams returned to their mosques that Friday, they communicated to their followers that "Islam lives deeply in Sekem in a way it does not exist anywhere else in the country." Those same imams gave Sekem "a plaque, written with beautiful calligraphy in golden letters, which states that the community of sheiks verify that Sekem is an Islamic initiative."

With the blessing of Islamic leaders,[3] Sekem thrived. What Abouleish, his family, and the community of Sekem workers overcame during the more than thirty years of development can hardly be overstated. Sekem leadership has consciously developed means for accessing human interconnections with nature while also using the best of modern science. One way they access human connections with nature comes through their experience with

---

3   Abouleish, *Sekem*, p. 149.

biodynamics, a method of agriculture that has received considerable notoriety in recent years with the high quality wines produced by biodynamic vineyards.

Biodynamic Agriculture: Old Knowledge in New Clothes. From the website of the Biodynamic Farming and Gardening Association, located in Oregon, biodynamic agriculture is described as combining organic farming methods with "consciousness of the uniqueness of each landscape," "working with nature's rhythms," perceiving "consciously and concretely the phenomena that induce life itself," and recognizing that "science is the practice of observing phenomena and relating them in a way that correctly represents the phenomena's reality."[4] It is regarded by some as the first modern ecological farming system and one of the most sustainable.[5]

The term *biodynamic* is a trademark held by the Demeter Association of biodynamic farmers for the purpose of maintaining production standards used both in farming and food processing. Demeter International, founded in Germany in 1928, is comprised of member countries each with its own Demeter organization required to meet international production standards. In France, for example, Biodivin certifies biodynamic wine. In Egypt, Sekem has created the Egyptian Biodynamic Association (EBDA), an association that provides training for farmers to become certified. The US Demeter Association was formed in the 1980s and certified its first farm in 1982.

Sekem is definitely not the first farming community to use a form of biodynamic agriculture, especially since biodynamic farming has much in common with other organic approaches. These approaches emphasize the use of manures and compost while excluding the use of artificial chemicals on soil and plants. Biodynamic agriculture adheres to these tenets but also uses fermented herbal and mineral

---

4   At http://www.biodynamics.com/biodynamics.

5   See for example Harwood, "A History of Sustainable Agriculture," in
     Edwards et al., *Sustainable Agricultural Systems*, pp. 3–19.

preparations in compost additives and field sprays, and follows an astronomical sowing and planting calendar.

A quick Internet search engine review reveals evidence of the similarities between biodynamic farming and farming with methods from indigenous peoples throughout the world, including Indians, Africans, Native Americans, and Indonesians. Dewane Morgan, a biodynamic farmer near Park Rapids, Minnesota, reported of a gathering he was invited to attend of native farmers from the Oneida, Ojibwe, Cheyenne, and Sioux tribes, a gathering rarely, if ever, attended by non-Native American farmers. He described conversations he had concerning how these farmers interacted with life forces of certain seeds to extend their quality and productivity, practices in keeping with biodynamics.[6]

For centuries, indigenous farmers have understood that certain natural phenomena like the movement of the planets and the moon affect long-term agricultural success. Sekem took this non-Enlightenment understanding and synthesized it with modern science—quality machinery for both production and processing—to create arguably the most effective sustainable farming system in the world. This type of synthesis is central to the New Enlightenment way of thinking and can serve as a benchmark for other Enlightenment thinkers to follow.

This discussion of Sekem and biodynamic agriculture provides an example of where human consciousness evolution is heading. Sekem's members are awake and aware to the type of full consciousness that is described in this chapter and following. In other words, members of the Sekem community understand both non-Enlightenment consciousness and the more recent self-consciousness arising from the Enlightenment. They understand how to "listen" and "connect" to nature while using beneficial modern technology.

---

6   Conversation with the author, Dec. 4, 2011.

An Enlightenment objection

One Enlightenment critique of Sekem and their use of biodynamics states that the reliance on astrological charts when planting amounts to magical thinking. Two problems exist with this critique. First, the Enlightenment perspective assumes there are no other avenues to knowledge beyond science, so they mistakenly conclude that astrological charts can have no bearing on farming efficacy. Second, many biodynamic researchers have applied scientific methodology to show the efficacy of following biodynamic astrological charts. It is helpful for the skeptical reader to understand that these astrological charts are not the same as those used to "read" people's horoscopes. Interested readers can refer to a number of biodynamic farming sites which discuss the use of astrological charts.[7] Therefore, the scientific method itself belies these critics' assertions.

One must ask what led indigenous farmers worldwide to understand the role of the moon and planets. One could argue that these farmers used trial and error and unwittingly discovered that the stars were in certain positions at certain times when their preparations became successful. Yet, indigenous farmers themselves say they either listen to the spirits of the environment talking to them or just "know" from their "read" of the environment.[8] One thing is certain: these methods "work." In this respect, one can conclude that they are scientific—the proof is in the pudding.

One of the challenges many Enlightenment thinkers must overcome is their assumption that access to knowledge outside of the channels of Enlightenment science are somehow illogical or irrational. These avenues to knowledge are not illogical when they can be seen from within the perspective of how the human mind works. The human mind has evolved to the place where we can now be more

---

7   Two places to begin are at http://science.howstuffworks.com/environmental /green-science/biodynamic-agriculture1.htm and http://goviya.com /biodynamic-farming.htm.

8   See, among others, http://www.intk.org/, http://fourbridges.farming, http://www.infrc.or.jp/english/KNF_Data_Base_Web/.../C2-4-033.pdf.

aware and perceptive of what exists. If a non-scientific approach to knowledge is legitimate, it will hold together when human reason is applied. But it has to be applied based on how *thinking* works, typically not done by critics who apply only a scientific framework. This should become more clear as we continue our journey in the pages ahead. Just before we start digging more deeply I want to address in the short section that follows what may arise in some readers' minds as a potential objection. This regards our view of comparing writings from various times and places.

The Right Way to Trace an Idea through History

In order to learn how to think differently, we must learn from the past. However, to do so we will need to correct an error common to those who interpret writings of pre-Enlightenment eras. The error occurs when considering the thought of great writers of the pre-Enlightenment era. One cannot simply take an idea and trace it. For example, the thinking goes: 1) Plato spoke a great deal about the state and government, as well as poetry and drama. 2) Other philosophers have discussed these subjects as well. 3) Therefore, we can learn by comparing what Plato thought with what other philosophers have said in order to see the similarities and differences.

This logic is flawed. Plato (and other pre-Enlightenment Scholastics such as Thomas Aquinas) did not live and think within an Enlightenment mindset. We assume pre-Enlightenment and Enlightenment philosophers asked themselves the same questions but found different answers to them. We assume comparing pre-Enlightenment thinkers to Enlightenment thinkers is an apples to apples comparison, when in fact it is apples to oranges. As an example, we find it convenient to take Plato and Aristotle's views regarding astrology and dismiss their thoughts as superstition common to their time. We forgive them but do not take them seriously. In doing so, we fail to understand what they meant by astrology within their non-Enlightenment consciousness. Their understanding of astrology was vastly different than ours. Whole realms of insight and knowledge have been lost owing to the fact that we interpret past philosophers from the Enlightenment perspective rather than from their unique non-Enlightenment perspective.

Learning to Read and Think Differently. One change that we can make is to apply careful and deliberate investigation of the avenues to knowledge. For those who wrote prior to the Enlightenment (or for contemporary writers from a non-Enlightenment worldview, such as portions of India and Asia), we must read from the point of view of their consciousness, a task that will take much more effort for those of us who have hardened habits of thought due to our language and education.

One result of this will be the ability to more effectively evaluate contemporary writers and gurus. We need to understand the theory of knowledge from which they have crafted their theories. If they do not know how to articulate their own theory of knowledge, it doesn't mean we automatically dismiss them. However, I do not believe that every writer or guru has some secret knowledge the world needs. There are wacky theories with no grounding in how humans actually come to understand anything. These need to be debunked, and will be, when we take into account the way the human mind creates meaning through the use of reason. In order to begin illustrating this, we will look closely at the phenomenon of sound.

How Thinking Happens: The Mockingbird

How do our minds convert the sensory data of any sound into meaning? Imagine you are hearing the sounds of a mockingbird for the very first time. Mockingbirds are known to make four distinct noises, each sounding like a separate bird (hence, "mocking" bird). If you have never heard a mockingbird or are unaware of its ability to sound like four different birds, you may be confounded when you hear it. What you "hear" are sound waves interacting with the cilia in your ear which communicates something about this energy to your mind. When you identify it, you are not using only your ears but also your mental habits, memory, imagination, feeling, and will. Using these "constructions" is vital to our perception of the world. Without them, we would be unable to identify, for example, the four unique sounds made by mockingbirds.

The following is an example of how we (as Enlightenment thinkers) might use these constructs to identify a mockingbird's sounds the first time we are exposed to them. I will proceed in the section that follows this one to describe how a non-Enlightenment thinker might experience the mockingbird. You will note the different ground of knowledge on which the two base their experience. This practice will be useful as it will help you begin to see the habits of thought that limit how you think. It will also shed light on how novelty and the conscious use of the imagination, key to the New Enlightenment, takes place.

An Enlightenment Thinker

You hear something. If your mind becomes aware of the sound, and you bring your awareness to focus on that sound, you will immediately begin unconsciously using constructs such as mental habits, memory, visualization, feelings, and the will. How you use each construct is discussed in turn below.

MENTAL HABITS: You cannot help but "think." You immediately use your learned analytical skills to start asking questions.

1. If I'm outside: Are there trees nearby?
2. If I'm inside a house or other structure: Are there windows open? Is a stereo playing those sounds?
3. I conclude: These types of sounds are generally made by birds. They have the right timbre and pitch to be birds. The volume of these sounds indicates to me that the birds must be close.

MEMORY: As you analyze the sounds, you jog your memory to see if you have experiences you can compare and contrast to this one.

- I've heard sounds just like these before, which I know to have been different types of birds
- But these sounds are strange because they keep changing from one type of bird to another to another yet seem to emanate from the same location
- I would not expect four different birds to be in the same place, all singing, and nothing in my memory allows me to conclusively determine what I am hearing

IMAGINATION: As you listen, you use your imagination and continue to analyze and visualize.

- I imagine the four birds sitting on various limbs on a tree or a couple of trees close by, sounding happy
- But it seems a bit odd to have that many birds in the same place
- Maybe only one bird is making all four of these sounds. How is that possible?

FEELING: Feelings play a role in your analysis.

- I feel curious
- I feel a sense of mystery
- I enjoy the variety but am surprised by the uniqueness of the experience

WILL: You determine to keep your awareness on the sound. This leads you to analyze and use your imagination because you are interested to do so. You focus your thoughts, feelings, and senses to help understand your situation.

- I keep clarifying that the sound comes from one location
- I'm still not sure how those four birds are all together in the same place; perhaps I am missing something? Maybe only one bird is making all of the sounds?

All of these constructs happen within micro-moments of hearing the bird sounds for the first time, yet in that time quite a bit of information is dissected and analyzed. If you have never heard a mockingbird before but find yourself in this situation with both the time and interest, you will use all of the above (mental habits, memory, imagination, feeling, will) to try and decipher how you heard four birds singing in one place. If you are able, you will likely walk out to where the sound comes from and attempt to locate the birds. Using your deductive abilities over the course of a few moments you will solve the riddle, and, for the first time, experience the amazing ability of a single mockingbird.

Reviewing what takes place:

1. Sound waves are produced by the singing of the mockingbird
2. You experience the sound waves through the cilia in your ears
3. This experience is transmitted to your mind via your nervous system and your brain
4. You use constructs learned throughout your life to determine the quandary of hearing four birds in the same place within milliseconds of hearing the sounds
5. You look for a cause of the sound

A Non-Enlightenment Thinker

The following is how a non-Enlightenment thinker might experience the sound of the mockingbird. Note how the experience is much like a fish in water, with no awareness of the water.

We do not immediately use logic to parse the sounds because such analytical thinking has yet to evolve. There are no questions because there is no "me" separate from the sound. We experience the unity of the forest and the tribal lands and our unity with all that exists. We feel the move of nature and understand this in our soul. Our knowing is in our being and our knowing flows out from our being and into our being and the being that is one. The sounds of the bird are a part of our tribe and we are part of it. The sounds reverberate within every part of our being. We are one with the sound. It does not matter whether we "recognize" the sounds as something we have heard before; all that matters is that these sounds communicate to me. They are a part of us and we are a part of them. There is no way to conceptually sever me as an "individual" from these sounds because both of us are a part of the same life force. We would not "imagine" a scene about where these birds might be perched; rather: We feel our tribe's force in conversation with the environment through these sounds. We do not experience curiosity or pleasure but an immediate connection; more like a union with the bird, so that the part that is "us" resolves into the environment and is one with it and the bird. We do not internally focus our attention since the power of our will is so weak that we cannot focus attention. Our attention is called forth by our surroundings. Our awareness is with the surroundings, not within ourselves.

As a non-Enlightenment thinker you do not look for causes. You do not possess a sharp incisive intellect to even consider looking for causes. What occurs in the world is a sense of one-ness. From the perspective of Enlightenment thinking it appears that the non-Enlightenment person is tossed and turned by the fates. The non-Enlightenment person does not feel this way for they have yet to isolate their individuality in such a way as to reflect on their state.

To look for a cause of something, you must *think*. Between the perception of sound and any kind of statement about it, as Austrian philosopher Rudolf Steiner says, "thinking inserts itself."[9] Without choosing to focus your thoughts the world would simply be a multiplicity of uniform objects. In this case you used your individual will to choose to focus on the bird sounds. Understand that there is a basic difference between a mental act and certain physical acts. If I slip on the snow and fall flat on my back, that is an unintentional physical act. But there is no such thing as an unintentional mental act. When you think, you choose to focus your mind. With all mental acts (thinking, wishing, loving, remembering) there is an element of will, of intentionality. It flows purposefully or not at all.

This element of will shows that we are not tossed and turned by the fates. It also shows that we are not merely the product of a

9   Steiner, *Intuitive Thinking as a Spiritual Path*, p. 79.

mechanistic, materialistic universe. We have freedom to focus our own thought. We have the ability to sustain a thought or change its direction as we choose. It is impossible to reduce that to a will-less mechanism. The freedom we have forms an important principle for the New Enlightenment theory of knowledge, a principle at odds with that implied by the Newtonian science of Enlightenment thinking.

The Birth of "Me." Simply being aware of and perceiving the mockingbird sounds is only one part of reality as we know it—the part divorced from individualistic analysis or logical deconstruction (i.e., what non-Enlightenment thinkers may perceive). The other part of reality that gives these sounds meaning occurs *within you* when you think about the perceptions. As you work to figure out the four bird sounds, you are the self-aware subject trying to determine whether there is either one bird or more than one. The unseen detective aiding you in solving the mockingbird mystery is your mind's thought processes. The ability for the average person to invoke these mental images and constructions is a result of Enlightenment evolution.

Take a moment to remember what was stated earlier: You exist as an object to yourself. You are able to "watch" yourself in your mind. Sometimes you likely surprise yourself with what you do, say or think. In a real way, *"you" exist as an individual because of thinking.* Were you not aware of yourself as a subject in your own mind, you would not consciously know there is a "you." You exist as both a subject and an object: a subject when you think of something other than yourself, and an object when you think about yourself. You, as a living breathing human individual, are living within the reality woven by thinking.

Some may object to the view that each experience must be driven by using thought constructs at all times. These people contend that thoughts are "stored" in your brain, much like bytes in a computer's circuits, and therefore there is no need to use thinking constructs in order to access this information. However, thoughts do not stay in your brain. Your brain is a physical organ, but it does not store perceptions and thought like a computer hard drive.

Despite the many efforts of science to locate color, sound, an idea, or a memory in the physical brain, none has been located. Scientists conclude that one cannot say where the sound (or color or idea) resides. These experiences reside in our mind, not our brain. Our mind does not reside in, nor is equivalent to, the gray matter of our physical brain. Our mind works through this physical organ. The brain serves more as a reflector of our minds, the physical matter through which we become conscious of our thoughts. Physical changes in the brain (stroke, injury, aging) affect *access* to our mind. I will not attempt to convince you of this at this point. Simply allow this idea to remain as you continue reading.

Thinking in a Non-Enlightenment Way. Let's return for a moment to the non-Enlightenment individual's description of the four different bird sounds. To review, you may think it odd to consider that people in non-Enlightenment times experienced a bird differently than we Enlightenment thinkers experience it. We see and experience a bird and see a detached *object*; a "representation." You see a bird, I see a bird, the person driving by sees a bird.

Non-scientific thinkers do not see a bird in the same way. They do not see things as objects separate from other objects. Rather, they see them as part of a living, three-dimensional fabric interconnected with everything around them. They do not separate the bird out as an object and view it in isolation from its environment. Their experience of the bird in connection with its environment has been termed a "synthetic experience" by cultural anthropologist Claude Levy-Bruhl.[10] For the non-Enlightenment person, all of an environment is primarily a unity or a synthesis—something primarily *felt*—rather than a collection of independent objects.

---

10   "It is not a question of association. The mystic properties with which things are imbued form an integral part of the idea to the primitive who views it as a synthetic whole. It is at a later stage of social evolution that what we call a natural phenomenon tends to become the sole content of perception to the exclusion of other elements which then assume the aspect of beliefs, and finally appear superstitious. But as long as this 'dissociation' does not take place, perception remains an undifferentiated whole." Claude Levy-Bruhl, quoted in Barfield, *Saving the Appearances*, p. 27.

If I ask you for your definition of a "bird," how do you respond? As one educated in the land of Enlightenment, you likely respond with something similar to "there are many flying objects with wings and they are all part of the same 'class' in the animal kingdom." Perhaps you are even aware that Carl Linnaeus was a Swedish scientist who established a hierarchy of living organisms so that scientists all over the world could understand each other. The system is still being used today though modifications of his original classifications of birds have taken place. The science of naming things, such as birds, called "taxonomy," can become quite complicated, but the basics are easy to understand. All birds are in the *Animalia* kingdom, the phylum of *Chordata* (with a backbone), and the class *Aves* (birds).

Non-Enlightenment thinkers do not have this type of organization in their heads. They do not even have the word *bird* in as we think of it when we say the term. Prior to sixteenth century, humans did not regularly classify and organize various objects into convenient groupings so they could be discussed. This human practice emerged as part of modern scientific thinking. Hence, their experience of the bird was much more immediate, intuitive, and unconscious.

A non-Enlightenment thinker sees and experiences a different world; one that is, in many important ways, deeper than our experience. But the person experiences it with a different consciousness, and consequently, with a different type of language. We have considerable difficulty, partly because of an assumption Westerners make, that we are more advanced than non-Enlightenment thinkers, communicating with those with a different consciousness.

Chichen Itza. The ancient Maya civilization gives us several examples of non-Enlightenment genius and suggests that many of their feats, especially certain structures, could not have been built but for their interconnectivity with the world around them. "El Castillo," a ninety-foot pyramid located in the Chichen Itza ruins in present day Yucatan, Mexico, is one example. The Maya built El Castillo sometime between the ninth and thirteenth centuries, both to honor the god Quetzalcoatl (meaning "serpent bird") and to create a physical manifestation of their solar calendar.

If one stands next to the structure and claps, the echo sounds exactly like the noise of a quetzal bird. Legend states that the god Quetzalcoatl wore a headdress created from hundreds of quetzal feathers, and so the quetzal has always had a mystical place in Maya lore. Maya used to gather by the thousands and clap in unison in worship.

Furthermore, the structure has four sides with ninety-one steps each; combined with the shared step at the top, there are exactly 365 steps on the structure, the number of days in a year. There are several other connections to their calendar manifested on El Castillo, but perhaps most impressive is the shadow display created on the pyramid's steps during both the vernal and autumnal equinoxes. The interplay between the sunlight and the edges of the steps on the pyramid create a shadow display on the northern stairway during which a jagged line of seven interlocking triangles appears to be a long tail leading downward to the carved stone head of the serpent Kukulkan, which resides at the base of the stairway. The snake's body appears only briefly, and only on the equinoxes—and has done so for a thousand years.

Of course, as many know, the Maya calendar—famous for its detailed accuracy—ends on December 21, 2012, the precise moment when the earth will have completed its 26,000-year procession and be exactly aligned with other planets in the Milky Way.

This type of seemingly impossible genius and architectural prowess without any advanced instruments of the twenty-first century can best be explained by the Maya's interconnectivity with the world around them. It is this type of non-Enlightenment interconnectivity our world needs to recapture.

Figuration. Another way to think about the differences between pre-logical and Enlightenment thinkers involves the use of the Barfieldian term *figuration.* Earlier in this chapter I explained that societies have collective representations of objects. The objects of nature appear to us as they do because of how we interact with the unrepresented subatomic world. Figuration is a term to convey the sum total of a society's collective representations. Non-Enlightenment people experienced the world in a different figuration than Enlightenment thinkers do. As humans evolved and, over time, became more individualistic, these ties to nature and to a social collective faded. A new figuration developed with the Enlightenment and replaced the natural figuration common to non-Enlightenment peoples.

As for our mockingbird: once we learn that the word *bird* means a sentient being with a backbone and is part of the bird (*Aves*) family, the next time we see and hear a mockingbird, we don't have to think about whether it is a bird or not. We already have that concept in our minds. It *is* a bird to us. For non-Enlightenment thinkers it is *not* a bird, nor is it a solo object. It is part of a system of meaning, connected in a synthesis, and part of a whole, whether totemic for their tribe, a harbinger of spring, or a warning of danger.

This is, understandably, a difficult concept to grasp and an even harder one for Enlightenment thinkers to believe. But, I would suggest we as Enlightenment thinkers are prejudiced because we think our way of viewing the bird is advanced and "better" than the non-Enlightenment thinker. In contrast, what has really happened is that we have lost the knowledge of the non-Enlightenment thinker. The two views are not contradictory but complementary. Wouldn't it be great if we could tap into the "mysterious" knowledge of seemingly-brilliant ancient civilizations like the Maya or the ancient Egyptians with their building of the pyramids or the astronomical insights of the builders of Stonehenge? The Enlightenment way of thinking need no longer relegate earlier ways of thinking to the history books; it need recognize its difference and seek to enter the consciousness of non-Enlightenment thinkers. The theory of knowledge of the New Enlightenment provides a way to synthesize the two ways of seeing so they can both be accessed and used, rather than strictly adhering to one or the other.

Awareness of the evolution of consciousness gives us the potential of developing an ability to know not only the scientific meaning that is natural to us, but the non-Enlightenment way as well. We can have the freedom to choose to use both. It is something we will have to learn and practice.

A Faulty Assumption

It is natural to struggle to understand how people at different times in human history see differently from one another. The fundamental reason we struggle to understand this is a mistaken assumption we have toward the "objects" that are part of our surroundings. We mistakenly believe that the psychological intersection, or nexus, between humanity and nature is the same now as it was when humans first appeared on earth. In short, we make the assumption that an oak tree, for example, looks the same to us as it did to humans thousands of years ago. It did not, and not because of minor evolutionary changes in the physical appearance of the tree itself. It does not look the same because the humans of thousands of years ago had a different figuration.

We are not the humans of thousands of years ago. Their knowledge of a tree was different; their assumptions about trees were different. Their experience as a human being was quite different than ours today. As a result, they experienced the tree differently, and, in some important respects, had more knowledge of the tree than we do today. The challenge of demonstrating this is summed up in the following passage from Barfield's *Saving the Appearances: A Study in Idolatry:*

> Those of the Middle Ages and their predecessors did indeed live in a different world from ours. The difficulties in the way of such a demonstration are very great, because it is the very nature of our own representations that they are fixed, as a sort of idol to which all representative significance is denied, and which cannot therefore (so it is felt) have altered merely with the alteration of human consciousness. Since it is, for us, a matter of "common sense," if not of definition, that phenomena are wholly

independent of consciousness, the impulse to ignore or explain away any evidence to the contrary is almost irresistible.

Yet, as with most inveterate prejudices, the reward of over-coming it requites the exertion. The idols are tough and hard to crack, but through the first real fissure we make in them we find ourselves looking, how deeply, into a new world!... With the first glimpse we now get of the familiar world and human history lying together, bathed in the light of the evolution of consciousness.[11]

We participate in producing the objects we perceive—in each and every act of human perception—for no one actually "sees" the subatomic particles that physics informs us are the ultimate con-stituent of reality. We have been educated and enculturated by our society to believe that all objects (nouns) and most of the processes of nature exist independent of ourselves. Barfield calls these inde-pendent objects/things "idols" because of the belief most of us have that objects are as they seem, always have been, and always will be. When we believe objects are objectively real without our participa-tion, we turn them into idols.

Correcting the Faulty Assumption. The following is a list of themes explicit in the Barfield passage above and some themes that follow from it. These form an important part of the New Enlightenment. This is also a good checkpoint along the path we have been traveling and the terrain we will travel in the pages ahead.

1. Humans were conscious of their world in a different way, during and preceding the Middle Ages, than we are today. Their experience with one another and with nature was qualitatively different
2. Our minds and our paths for thinking—in essence, our consciousness—have evolved in discernible ways, and continue to evolve

---

11   Barfield, *Saving the Appearances*, p. 78.

3. There is great value in gaining a correct mental picture of the past, as it will help our awareness of where we are today and, thus, help us better shape the future. Our understanding of the past is skewed, particularly by the mistaken "assumption" described above, that an experience of the earth a millennia ago is fundamentally the same as an experience of the earth today

4. We have much to overcome in order to understand the significance of the differences between our knowledge and non-Enlightenment knowledge: Our own understanding of the familiar world is set in such a way that we have a difficult time understanding how anyone could "see" the world any differently than we do. Coupled with this, we may have an underlying fear of the unfamiliar

5. The species *Homo sapiens* has become more individuated: Our consciousness (compared with the Middle Ages) is more *self*-aware than *group* consciousness

6. By breaking the hold that the idols have on our way of thinking we will experience a freedom and a joy of entering, as it were, a new world—one that always existed but of which we have not had the eyes with which to see

Most of us today view history of human thought primarily as past knowledge only useful for the bookshelf. One of the ways Barfield strongly influenced C. S. Lewis when they were both young college students concerned the high value Barfield placed on knowledge of non-Enlightenment humans and his understanding that when Plato, for example, was discussing ideas he was coming from a different consciousness than typical Westerners. Many current scholars of history project back in time, interpreting the writings of the past as if those writers were living in the same world of subjects and objects of which we are so habituated in the Enlightenment era. Barfield shows that the widespread taken-for-granted view of historians and philosophers that Plato viewed objects of sense perception as having an independent existence apart from the act of perception is simply not true, and is an example of "projecting post-logical thoughts back into a pre-logical age."[12] Were scholars to understand better the development and changes in language and words and the evolution of consciousness undertaken within Western society, they would avoid this flaw and find much from which to learn.

The Value of History. Too many modern scientific thinkers dismiss history as of little value and consequence in solving world issues. I hinted at this earlier in chapter 1 where I spoke of the sense most Enlightenment thinkers have that we are constantly improving on the past. This implies that we have little to learn from the past. In contrast, we have a great deal we can learn from history and have barely begun to do so.

A short examination of history as a discipline can help make this point. History did not become a discipline of study until the nineteenth century. Prior to this time, no one studied history for history's sake. Previous histories, such as that of the famous first century Jewish historian Josephus or ancient Greek's Herodotus, concerned only parochial history, not human history. The new interest in history as a study of humanity and its civilizations in the nineteenth century paralleled the excitement for science in the seventeenth century when it exploded onto the research scene.

However, nineteenth-century history mistakenly believed it could apply scientific methods to its study. The difficulty of doing this seems obvious today. The materials of study are vastly different. For the study of history, historians turn to records (mostly written) of the past. The raw materials of study are words, and often words written or spoken by those who were merely giving an account of an event. For science, of course, the raw materials of study are physical objects or processes, whether organic or inorganic, that theoretically can be handled and/or tested. One cannot effectively "test" words written about a past event.

As Barfield reminds us in several places, history, by definition, involves the presence of some sort of human intention and

---

12   Barfield, *Poetic Diction*, p. 194.

individual thought or of thoughts entertained by an individual mind. For example, Alexander the Great's conquest of much of the known world, or the 9/11 bombings of New York City's World Trade Center, certainly involved human intention and thought. The individuals participating in these events, with their thoughts and intentions, exemplify the "inside" of the events. In fact, one cannot study history without studying it from the inside. What is history if not for the thoughts and intentions behind its stories?

To study history one reenacts the events by thinking the same thoughts as those who were part of the events. It is a reconstruction of the past in the imagination of the present. All study of history requires the use of the imagination. We look back into it not onto it. And, as we will learn later, imagination becomes a valued skill for helping educating future generations into the New Enlightenment.

As to the relation between nature and history, anything that precedes human intention and thought comes under the heading of nature and not History. Nature can involve instinctive human behavior, but not thoughtful human behavior. History is primarily the history of thought. And as we will see in the next chapter, language and words prompt the creation of the thoughts and ideas we share with one another.

Summary

To begin this book's presentation of the theory of knowledge behind the New Enlightenment, I introduced "The Belief," followed by an explanation of the limitations of classic science and the Trojan Horse embedded within. Subsequently, I introduced and outlined the concept of human consciousness evolution and the idea that, in order to continue our evolution of consciousness, it is necessary to learn a different way to think—in essence, a different way of seeing and experiencing the macro-world within which we spend our day. I provided some examples of what non-Enlightenment humans experienced in life to help illustrate different ways of thinking.

At various points I mentioned the fact that the issue of language, particularly the subject–object divide, shapes our Enlightenment way of thinking. To this topic we turn.

Chapter 5

CONSCIOUSNESS AND LANGUAGE

"Language is central to our experience of being human, and the languages we speak profoundly shape the way we think, the way we see the world, the way we live our lives."
—LERA BORODITSKY[1]

*"The **most** fundamental assumption of any age are those that are implicit in the meanings of its common words.[2]... In our language alone, not to speak of its many companions, the past history of humanity is spread out in an imperishable map, just as the history of the mineral earth lies embedded in the layers of its outer crust.... Language has preserved for us the inner, living history of our soul. It reveals the evolution of consciousness.*
—OWEN BARFIELD[3]

Language can be described as the prison where we live, but it is also the way we "clarify life's confusing blur...cage flooding emotions [and]...coax elusive memories....We don't really know what we think, how we feel, what we want, or even who we are until we struggle to find the 'right words.'"[4] Changes in language lead to changes in thinking and, consequently, changes in our perception of the world. As we penetrate the veil of language's dominating influ-

---

1   Boroditsky, http://www.edge.org/3rd_culture/boroditsky09/boroditsky09 _index.html.

2   Barfield, *Speaker's Meaning*, p. 26.

3   Barfield, *History in English Words*.

4   Ackerman, *Deep Play*, pp. 121–122.

ence on our perceptions, we can observe within ourselves how it shapes our very thoughts.

Language is not like an unchanging computer programming language. Rather, it evolves and morphs, oscillating as it were between the poles of logic and creativity. Meaning is created, and, from another perspective, meaning is revealed, through changes in language. The study of language and its changes is the study of consciousness and its evolution. Through this study we may be able to rediscover the insides of the world we tend to see only as outer surfaces of matter.

How Language Affects What We Perceive

Lera Boroditsky, assistant professor of psychology, neuroscience, and symbolic systems at Stanford University, has written extensively about how languages affect the way we think. The following, an extended passage from one of her on-line postings, demonstrates how even the smallest nuances of language affect how people perceive both their environment and their perspective on life:

> For a long time, the idea that language might shape thought was considered at best untestable and more often simply wrong. Research in my labs at Stanford University and at MIT has helped reopen this question. We have collected data around the world: from China, Greece, Chile, Indonesia, Russia, and Aboriginal Australia. What we have learned is that people who speak different languages do indeed think differently and that even flukes of grammar can profoundly affect how we see the world.... Even what might be deemed frivolous aspects of language can have far-reaching subconscious effects on how we see the world.
>
> Take grammatical gender. In Spanish and other Romance languages, nouns are either masculine or feminine. In many other languages, nouns are divided into many more genders ("gender" in this context meaning class or kind).
>
> What it means for a language to have grammatical gender is that words belonging to different genders get treated

differently grammatically and words belonging to the same grammatical gender get treated the same grammatically. Languages can require speakers to change pronouns, adjective and verb endings, possessives, numerals, and so on, depending on the noun's gender. For example, to say something like "my chair was old" in Russian (*moy stul bil' stariy*), you'd need to make every word in the sentence agree in gender with "chair" (*stul*), which is masculine in Russian. So you'd use the masculine form of "my," "was," and "old." These are the same forms you'd use in speaking of a biological male, as in "my grandfather was old." If, instead of speaking of a chair, you were speaking of a bed (*krovat'*), which is feminine in Russian, or about your grandmother, you would use the feminine form of "my," "was," and "old."

Does treating chairs as masculine and beds as feminine in the grammar make Russian speakers think of chairs as being more like men and beds as more like women in some way? It turns out that it does. In one study, we asked German and Spanish speakers to describe objects having opposite gender assignment in those two languages. The descriptions they gave differed in a way predicted by grammatical gender. For example, when asked to describe a "key"—a word that is masculine in German and feminine in Spanish—the German speakers were more likely to use words like "hard," "heavy," "jagged," "metal," "serrated," and "useful," whereas Spanish speakers were more likely to say "golden," "intricate," "little," "lovely," "shiny," and "tiny." To describe a "bridge," which is feminine in German and masculine in Spanish, the German speakers said "beautiful," "elegant," "fragile," "peaceful," "pretty," and "slender," and the Spanish speakers said "big," "dangerous," "long," "strong," "sturdy," and "towering." This was true even though all testing was done in English, a language without grammatical gender. The same pattern of results also emerged in entirely nonlinguistic tasks (e.g., rating similarity between pictures). And we can also show that it is aspects of language per se that shape how people think: teaching English speakers new grammatical gender systems influences mental representations of objects in the same way it does with German and Spanish speakers. Apparently even small flukes of grammar, like the seemingly arbitrary assignment of gender to a noun, can have an effect on people's ideas of concrete objects in the world.[5]

In fact, you don't even need to go into the lab to see these effects of language; you can see them with your own eyes in an art gallery. Look at some famous examples of personification in art—the ways in which abstract entities such as death, sin, victory, or time are given human form. How does an artist decide whether death, say, or time should be painted as a man or a woman? It turns out that in eighty-five percent of such personifications, whether a male or female figure is chosen is predicted by the grammatical gender of the word in the artist's native language.... The fact that even quirks of grammar, such as grammatical gender, can affect our thinking is profound...

Other studies have found effects of language on how people construe events, reason about causality, keep track of number, understand material substance, perceive and experience emotion, reason about other people's minds, choose to take risks, and even in the way they choose professions and spouses.[6] Taken together, these results show that linguistic processes are pervasive in most fundamental domains of thought, unconsciously shaping us from the nuts and bolts of

---

5   L. Boroditsky et al., "Sex, Syntax, and Semantics," in Gentner and Goldin-Meadow, *Language in Mind*, pp. 61–79.

6   L. Boroditsky, "Linguistic Relativity," in Nadel, *Encyclopedia of Cognitive Science*, pp. 917–921; B. Pelham et al., "Why Susie sells seashells by the seashore: Implicit egotism and major life decisions," *Journal of Personality and Social Psychology* 2002, 82(4):469–86; Tversky and Kahneman, "The Framing of decisions and the psychology of choice," *Science* 1981, 211:453–58; P. Pica et al., "Exact and approximate arithmetic in an Amazonian Indigene group," *Science* 2004, 306:499–503; de Villiers and de Villiers, "Linguistic Determinism and False Belief," in Mitchell and Riggs, *Children's Reasoning and the Mind*; Lucy and Gaskins, "Interaction of language type and referent type in the development of nonverbal classification preferences," in Gentner and Goldin-Meadow, *Language in Mind*, pp. 465–92; Barrett et al., "Language as a context for emotion perception," *Trends in Cognitive Sciences* 2007, 11:327–332.

cognition and perception to our loftiest abstract notions and major life decisions.[7]

Boroditsky's finding is both fascinating and provocative. It helps illustrate the influence languages have in how each of us perceives what is around us.

Another brief example that illustrates this point comes from Nobel Laureate in Medicine (1987) Susumu Tonegawa, who stated that the Japanese language is not suited for scientific research. "We [Japanese] should consider changing our thinking process in the field of science by trying to reason in English."[8] By this, he was not suggesting the superiority of English but, rather, asserting that Western languages have a precision that makes them ideal for scientific thinking.

The Roles of Language

Language has two main roles. Its primary role is that of revealing, of allowing things to appear. Its secondary role is that of representation or labeling. Our Enlightenment "common sense" would say that labeling is its primary role and that one of the goals educating children is to help them learn the labels.

Our confusion stems from the view we have that says our mind is in our heads and everything else is "out there." This mistaken view says the purpose of education is to recognize the object "out there" and then label it. But by the time we have recognized the object the cognition process is completed and we are left with a mental picture of, for example, a table, in our mind. We do not notice the active moment of cognition. The cognition process is over by the time we notice anything.

You can only recognize a table when you have the concept of table already in your mind. The concept of table constitutes the table. As Henri Bortoft explains, "We can recognize *any* table

---

7   Boroditsky, at http://www.edge.org/3rd_culture/boroditsky09 /boroditsky09_index.html.

8   Cited in Postman, *Technopoly*, p. 124.

in the first place only by means of the concept, i.e., the "table" idea. To be able to see *one* table is already to be able to see all tables, i.e., all *possible* tables."[9] The *table* concept is active; it is not simply a mental picture of a table. It creates all possible tables. When you have a mental picture you are already one step removed from the process of the creation of the table. If you do not have the "*table* concept," you would encounter some materials arranged in a manner that would leave you confused. It is only when the *table* concept fuses with your perception that you actually experience a table. Otherwise you experience some odd arrangement of materials.

It requires us going to the exact moment of forming the perception of the table to see that this moment is where the creation of the table occurs. The table is not already there until the *table* concept actively connects with our sensory input to create the table. There are too many examples to prove my point but I would remind you of my earlier reference to deaf and blind people who had their loss of a sensory organ restored and experienced dramatic confusion when faced with sensory input. They did not have the concept needed to create the meaning that you or I take for granted. For an in-depth view of this, I refer you to the writings of Oliver Sacks, particularly *The Man Who Mistook His Wife for a Hat*.

We fail to see what takes place at that creative instant when a word-concept brings into being the thing that appear to us. It is the moment of organizing the unrepresented through using a word-concept that allows appearance to occur. The magic is in the language. Philosopher Martin Heidegger referred to this as a "saying which is showing,"[10] meaning that language and the concepts it provides structures our inner worlds into objects, phenomena, and meaning. Linguistic theorist Hans Gadamer said it this way: "Being[11] that can be understood is Language."[12]

---

9 Bortoft, *The Wholeness of Nature*, p. 133.

10 Heidegger, *On the Way to Language*, pp. 134–136.

11 Or "existence."

12 Gadamer, *Truth and Method*, p. 474.

The other aspect of the table example is that the act of seeing the table is the primary occurrence that leads to the "seeing person" and the "seen object." The person-subject and table-object are not independent of one another. They form either end of a polarity which requires both ends to have the event of table-appearing to occur.

This explanation generally is difficult for most of us Enlightenment thinkers. Be patient with yourself as you work on gaining insight into a very different consciousness from what we have all been raised to have. It may help to contrast these ideas with the common theories of language in the West.

Enlightenment and Postmodern Theories of Language

Previously, I wrote extensively about Enlightenment thinking and its corresponding result, "The Belief." Enlightenment thinking views words and concepts as either:

1) emotive—an abstract word with no physical referent, or
2) referential—"true," or veridical (demonstrable), since it has a physical referent

The only "meanings" you can confidently discuss with this theory are the meanings that correspond to physical referents such as events or objects. This theory, if followed, eliminates meanings associated with many abstract words in our language including, ironically, the words emotive, referential, and veridical. Theorists who articulate this point of view attempt to eliminate all propositions except those that can be deduced from observation.

Enlightenment thinkers often cite philosopher David Hume for support. He asserted that the ideas we have in our head are produced via our *passive* reception of impressions from the sense data caused by objects. It is as if sensory data presses in on our brain and leaves its imprint. Consequently, the ideas in our head are leftovers from what we've touched, smelled, seen, tasted, and heard. This has become the "common sense" view of Westerners, given that most of us have not analyzed how meaning occurs in our minds.

Postmodern Critique of "Modernity." Postmodernism arose during the middle to end of the twentieth century and can be seen as a critique of modernity (their term for Enlightenment thinking), particularly in the area of language. Postmodernists place emphasis on the plurality of meaning—instead of a search for "the" meaning of something—while denying any universal purpose for humanity. The roots of postmodern theory began with criticisms of Enlightenment thinking. Postmodernism and its development as a philosophy received a major boost as a result of quantum physics' discoveries. Postmodernists use these discoveries as evidence supporting their view that reality has no meaning in and of itself. Many of the postmodern criticisms of modernity pointed to the same flaw explained in chapter 2, that scientific thinking is not the purely objective endeavor it purported to be in the Enlightenment mindset.

In place of the materialist point of view seen in Enlightenment thinkers, postmodernists emphasize the issues of the dynamics of power and control between and among individuals and institutions.[13] One example of this is feminism and women's rights. Postmodern researchers in the late twentieth century demonstrated that men exercise power and control over women through often unexpressed or unseen interpersonal dynamics. The critiques generated by these studies have influenced public policy and helped bring about moves toward equality between men and women in the workplace.

Words Used for Power and Control. Unlike Enlightenment thinkers, postmodernists view the world as containing no underlying substance or reality. The consequence of this view is that all "referents" in language are eliminated. They posit that attempts to claim truth through connections with physical realities are meaningless. A word, then, does not refer to some *thing* any longer. Certain words, and language in general, are often used as means for influence, power

---

13 The best-known seminal Postmodernist, Michel Foucault, wrote numerous
    works on institutionalized power and control.

and control, among and between individuals, societies, families, nations, institutions, and other social groupings.

My own research allows me to appreciate the insight postmodernists have given to societal power structures. They raise important issues. But I have been frustrated with postmodernism. It is as if they saw the flaws in modernity and chose to identify them without effectively articulating an alternative theory of knowledge that could be incorporated into Western education to move beyond the Enlightenment theory. Many postmodernists champion for the underdog based on an ethical system they cannot effectively articulate, since they do not speak effectively concerning the origin of their, or anyone else's, morality and ethics. Their discussions of this topic are either missing or explained simply by reference to power structures (such as a religion designing a moral framework) that serves to keep the structure in power and authority. This leads to their conclusion that any moral view becomes merely one competing point of view among many.

Concerning the issue of meaning, postmodernists speak of how individuals can interpret sense data in their own ways in order to create meaning for themselves. However, postmodernists, like the modernists they wish to replace, fail to effectively analyze the process of *how* individuals create meaning out of sense data. It is as if this question is not of concern. Their epistemology goes no further than the modernists.

Language and Knowledge

> Modern languages are fossil beds of such ancient unity, and abstract prose requires these inexhaustible fossils for its meaning. Poetry revivifies the metaphors.[14]

As the quotation from Terence Hipolito above states, language provides the fossil bed from which we can dig and discover changes in meaning and consciousness over time. Careful mining of non-Enlightenment writings and thought, along with the creative

---

14   Hipolito, "Owen Barfield's Poetic Diction" (*Renascence* 46, 1993).

imagination of "poets," can bring life to the metaphors and a rediscovery of the meaning and unity experienced by non-Enlightenment
thinkers. As well, interactions and collaborations with non-Enlightenment thinkers will contribute to this goal.

I spoke in chapter 3 about the dramatic increase in the number
of nouns in the English language and the way that ancient Greek
and other indigenous languages provide pathways for thinking in
more of what we could call a process-focused way. This change
illustrates an evolution in language. The increase of nouns cor-
responds to an increase in abstraction, an important point that
needs expansion. I will begin by explaining what is meant by
abstraction and then discuss how languages evolve and change
over time. In the process of doing so I will demonstrate how this
meaning has been fossilized and how it can be resuscitated, this
time in a conscious way.

Abstraction. To abstract is literally to take something away or to
separate something from its context. It's very similar to the word
extract. But "why would you want to take something away from its
context?" Physicist David Bohm responds:

> This is what thought is always doing. It picks on something
> that seems to be relevant and important and tries to discuss
> this in the abstract, because that simplifies it and enables us
> to focus on the main point. The opposite of the abstract is the
> concrete. The word concrete comes from the Latin word con-
> cresent, meaning "grown together." You may imagine a jungle
> with a vast amount of concrete reality. You are generally, how-
> ever, interested not in the whole jungle, but rather in certain
> animals or certain plants. In your mind you abstract a plant out
> of that vast jungle and say, "My mind is on that plant, I want to
> find that plant, because I want to eat it." You can see here the
> importance of abstraction. Even animals must abstract what is
> relevant in this jungle.
>   Reality is everything concrete and is much too much to be
> grasped by the mind in detail, so you make abstractions—call

that foreground—and leave the rest as background, which you don't notice very much. In this process of abstraction, the word calls attention to something and gives it shape. For example, we have a very patterned carpet here in this room. Once I lost a coin on this carpet and couldn't see it. But I saw a glint, and as soon as I saw this I saw the coin. The glint enabled me to abstract the coin from the carpet; otherwise, it was lost in the details of the pattern.

We are constantly even in such elementary ways using abstractions, and we build on that. Indeed, every name is an abstraction of a class or category like water, air, fire. Even the name of a person is an abstraction—it doesn't tell you all about the person; you usually associate with it a few things about that person.

Knowledge is built up from such abstractions, which are then abstracted yet further. For example, you have chairs, tables, bookcases, and you abstract that as furniture. You can abstract the furniture further as material objects, and you can go on in this way to more and more general abstractions. This hierarchy of abstractions enables you to reason.[15]

Without abstractions we couldn't function; thought would be of limited use. Abstracting allows you to leave out the vast complexity (i.e., the concrete unity that would be overwhelming).

Note the clear relation between words and abstraction. Words, when used with generally the same meaning by many people, are *things become*. They are established; they have been abstracted. This allows the words to be given an order so that logic can develop and they can be talked about between people. Heidegger describes the abstraction process as "an opening in a chaotic forest where there is, suddenly and inexplicably, clarity—a place where 'beings' are recognizable."[16] Language, in essence, names these beings and projects them into the clearing.[17]

---

15   Bohm, *Unfolding Meaning.*

16   Heidegger, *Poetry, Language, Thought*, p. 73.

17   Hipolito, "Owen Barfield's Poetic Diction" (*Renascence* 46, 1993) p. 12.

It may also help in thinking about abstractions to realize that we often mistakenly read abstract thought into the minds of children. Barfield uses the example of a daughter's name for her father. For a young child, "Dad" is only reserved for one dad, hers. Until she becomes old enough she has no concept of "dad-ness"—the abstraction that allows the word "dad" to refer to any father. This example of the practice of reading abstract thought into the minds of children is similar, by the way, to how we often read our subject/object world back into the minds of non-Enlightenment humanity who do not have that type of consciousness.

Limits of Abstractions. Abstractions can also be significantly limiting. Because abstractions give the impression of an independent existent reality, most of us fall into the habit of believing that our abstractions are "all there is." We have created a complex world based on the abstractions of thought and fail to remember that these abstractions were extracted from the concrete unity that is the interconnection of all of life.

Take the example of "tree." Using abstract thought we objectify sense impressions that share certain common characteristics: "I see a tall organized organic mass growing out of the ground with bark and branches and leaves. I call it a tree. Near it is another tall organic mass growing out of the ground with bark and so on that I call a tree." In this way we logically classify our sensory impressions, allowing us to communicate with others who share the meaning of the word "trees." We extract "trees" from the environment so that we can talk about them and perhaps do something (i.e., "clear the trees" so a house can be built).

But there is another part of the situation, and that is that the trees are embedded in a much larger ecosystem. They are home for a myriad of species of bugs, bacteria, animals, and the like and are interconnected under the ground with many other trees via their root system. It is endemic to the nature of abstraction to think about the abstraction mechanically, to think of it as a tree only in the sense of doing something with it. We make it an "it."

We struggle to consider the concrete unity from which we have extracted the object. Considering the larger ecosystem requires much effort on our part, and our knowledge of the large system is extremely limited relative to how much we know of the "parts" of the system.

The loss of knowledge of the concrete unity is the crux of the problem of Enlightenment thinking and its highly evolved abstractions. It is not that abstractions themselves are a problem; it is the fact that we have left behind knowledge of the unity, a knowledge which non-Enlightenment humans lived within, though unconsciously. We need to bring consciousness to this and rediscover the concrete unity—i.e., "revivify[ing] the metaphors." Understand, abstracting is a blessing in that, without the subject/object distinction that comes from abstract thinking, we would not be individuals. It is also a curse, however, because it involves experiencing nature not as a nursing mother or benevolent companion, but as an inhuman and meaningless mechanism. [18]

Another limit of our unconscious use of abstractions exemplifies "The Belief" discussed earlier. "The Belief" becomes the software program that responds to the situation. It does a lot for us but also limits us. It allows us to work with nature but does not help us understand how our thinking combines with the unrepresented to produce nature. For that, we need the higher sort of intelligence that we learn through penetrating the mystery of thinking. It is possible to think in a way that allows us to maintain the benefits we receive from the abstraction of language, while simultaneously learning to "read" nature for its holistic relationships.

How Language Changes: A Shift in Consciousness

In order to more completely understand how language shapes our thinking, we need to answer additional questions: How is language formed in the first place?[19] How does meaning "increase"

---

18   See Barfield's article "Participation and Isolation: A Fresh Light on Present Discontents," in *The Rediscovery of Meaning*.

19   For this question I refer you to Barfield, who spends time on this question in

or perhaps "decrease"? Who changes language? For the second two questions, consider the fact that we all have experienced change in language when we encounter new ideas and new meaning, an experience that, if meaningful, causes pleasure. Historically, the study of the experience of this effect dates back to the ancient Greeks in the discipline known as aesthetics, referring to the heightened sense of beauty that produces pleasure. You can actually experience a shift in your own consciousness by paying attention to the subjective physical and mental effects you experience when "moved" by poetry or by the addition of meaning to already-known words or concepts. The pleasure of appreciation takes place at the actual moment of change.

Consider how you feel when you are wrapped up in—lost in—either a new idea, a sublime piece of music, a sporting activity, or an unexpected, completely illuminating, plot moment in a movie. The moment you "come to yourself" and reflect on what you experienced gives insight into the experience of this pleasure. Changes in words and their meanings provide this, albeit in a more subtle way, but one that has significant consequences for how we "see" the world.

Perhaps you can remember when you were a small child and for the first time came in contact with certain words that intrigued you. I can remember when I understood "mystery" and "mischievous" for the first time. The realization of the words' meanings provided me a virginal sense of pleasure, a sense of entering into a new space. It gave me a palpable sense of fascination as my imagination was fired. Later I had the experience of using the words for the first time with someone else: "He sure is a mischievous dog," and "How she did that jump is a mystery." In that moment I briefly renewed the original sense of pleasure. The sense of pleasure dissipated through continued use of the word, though its original pleasure, its magic in revealing a new world, remains latent. This example is relevant because it gives insight into how

---

his book *History in English Words.*

meaning changes and how consciousness evolves through changes in language.

Changes in Words. Words are constantly changing because of the discrepancy between the lexical (dictionary) meaning of words and a speaker's meaning. As Barfield indicates, were there to be perfect (or pure) communication, the meanings of words would never change. Theoretically, everyone could learn the lexical meanings and we could all go merrily on our way, clearly communicating and clearly understanding. The ability for such precise communication would solve a lot of problems. Think of the marriages that would be saved and the misunderstandings that would be averted.

However, this state would cause more problems than we realize. What we would give up is the creative expression of an individual soul. It is through these expressions that new understandings and their resultant new meanings arise. To give an example, when Isaac Newton used the word *gravity* for the first time, it was a metaphorical use of the term, and consequently, expansive and creative in meaning. Previously, it meant only "heaviness." Newton would not have been able to "discover" gravity in the way that we think about it were the only type of communication possible pure communication.

Pure communication forms one pole in the polarity with the expressive/creative use of words. Through the expressive/creative pole, Newton adopted and adapted the word "gravity" to describe the natural process we all now know, conventionally, as gravity. For us today, the term has lost all metaphorical connotations. It has, in a sense, become hardened in meaning.[20] Such is the path of many of our words. As a portion of the Barfield quotation at the beginning of the chapter indicates, *"The most fundamental assumption of any age are those that are implicit in the meanings of its common words."*

---

20   Barfield, *Speaker's Meaning*, pp. 23-26.

Polarities. Polarities are unions of contraries, or as Aristotle is credited with saying, "The union of opposites is one." A polarity differs from a dichotomy in that a dichotomy consists of opposites that simply contradict each other, ensuring we can have one or the other but not both at the same time, whereas a polarity involves a necessary interdependence. A polarity is actually a unity. A physical example of a polarity is electricity—it exists because of the inter-connection between the positive and negative poles. Another example is water, which is neither oxygen nor hydrogen. Water is not the mere juxtaposition of corpuscles separated by invisible interspaces. It is dynamic, not abstract. It is living and generative interpenetration—generative of each other and generative of new product. The pole of pure communication and expression/creation form such a unity. Meaning is formed, as with electricity, on the tension between the two poles.

Humanity's mental and material progress—i.e. any additional growth in knowledge and understanding via language—is associated with expansion of meaning. The polarity between the lexical, or given, meaning of a word and how it comes to be used expressively and creatively forms the tension through which new meaning arises or lost meaning is rediscovered. If we work at it, this process will enable us to rediscover the knowledge of the concrete unity.

How Languages Evolves: The Poetic Becomes Prose. French philosopher Jacques Derrida made the statement that "history is the history of philosophy...(which is) the history of prose; or rather the becoming-prose of the world."[21] His phrase "becoming prose" signifies the abstraction process described above. Encountering new thought through language usage strikes us with its poetic nature. We experience a shift in our own consciousness. As this language usage becomes routine, we lose the poetic impact of the terms and ideas (think of Newton's "gravity," and "mischievous" and "mystery" from above).

---

21 Derrida, *Of Grammatology*, p. 287.

The way new words and meaning come about in a language can be seen by looking at the history of language change. In doing so we find two main vehicles: 1) When the people who speak a language encounter those who speak other languages, and, 2) as individuals reveal new meaning and introduce the new meaning to the language.

(1) *Encountering other languages.* In *History in English Words*, Barfield reviews how Indo-European languages developed and evolved through the migrations of two main groups of Aryan nomads who began with a common language. Shared words can be found in the languages of the Greek, Egyptian, Roman, Celtic, Persian, and Indian peoples to name a few. Similarities between Celtic and French, for example, also exist. These similarities arise once people who speak different languages begin to interact. Pre-interaction writings reveal zero shared words; post-interaction writings suddenly include a variety of shared words. In this way, where nothing or little exists in the archaeological ruins, words reveal lifestyle, thought, and patterns of migration. They allow the researcher to follow the movement of the precursor civilizations across Asia and Europe.

(2) *The revelation of meaning.* Many individuals have become quite adept at expressing and creating new meaning within words. Barfield calls these individuals poets, though by the term he does not limit the designation to those who only write poetry. Many of our great scientists have been "poets" in this way. They used their imagination to open the core of part of nature's mysteries and found innovative ways to reveal their discoveries through the language of their time. We must seek the mysteries behind their creativity and learn how to teach and inspire succeeding genera-tions with the expressive/creative pole of language. The dominat-ing emphasis brought about by "The Belief" dampens the creative spirit and makes it much easier for totalitarianism to rear its demonic head.

Metaphor, the Bridge to Discovering Meaning. Scientists and poets use metaphors to illuminate their discovered or rediscovered meaning. Metaphors work by looking through a conventional meaning to see the speakers' formative (creative) meaning. It is as if you see through the original word and understand the additional meaning or change in meaning presented by the speaker. Eventually the new meaning becomes standard as the translucence dims over time, eventually ceasing to become translucent. This demonstrates the essential historical nature of language. The true nature of language cannot be grasped without the recognition of this time dimension.

As an example, all of our words for mental processes—i.e. grasp, conceive, understand, attitude, conceive, focus, and the like—can be traced back to a material process. When the words were first used, they were metaphorical. "Grasp," the holding of something, is an easy one to grasp. Likewise we conceived children before we conceived concepts. Others take a little digging to solidly "stand under," but when you take the time to "focus" the lens you can "see" it.

Over time we no longer view a word metaphorically. Eventually the immaterial meaning of a word becomes the only meaning. Emerson pointed out, in a quotation similar to the one of Terence Hipolito's previously, that this is how the greater part of our vocabulary has been produced. He wrote:

> As the limestone of the continent consists of infinite masses of
> the shells of animalcules, so language is made up of images, or
> tropes, which now, in their secondary use, have long ceased to
> remind us of their poetic origin.[22]

Another key word illustrating this theme is *subjective,* or *subjectivity.* During the seventeenth century, the Oxford Dictionary defined *subjective* as "pertaining to the essence or reality of a thing; real, essential." In 1815, the definition changed to "having its source in the mind"; in 1890, it changed to "pertaining or

---

22 Emerson, *Essays,* 2nd series.

peculiar to an individual subject or his mental operations…personal, individual"; and by 1890, the definition changed even further to "existing in the mind only, without anything real to correspond with it; illusory, fanciful."

These changes demonstrate "The Belief" as it came to take hold in the nineteenth century as a world of objects existing chronologically prior to any person—i.e. the belief that the immaterial world exists and runs on without human beings. This consequence of "The Belief" shows that Enlightenment thinking has forgotten that the concept of an object without a subject is as abstract as the concept of a surface without a depth and as futile as that of a back without a front or a fiddle without a bow.

Contraction of Language. Language not only is constantly expanding, it is also constantly contracting. C. S. Lewis points out in his *Studies in Words* that many of our common words have contracted in meaning. He uses the example of "furniture." For almost all English speakers today, we assume this means something like movable articles, such as tables, chairs, desks, or cabinets used in homes and offices. However, three hundred years ago it carried meaning that allowed one writer to use the words "all the choir of heaven and furniture of earth." We would assume that to be a metaphorical meaning today, when in fact it preceded our current meaning and could not be metaphorical in that way. It is an example of a word, one of many thousands, that has contracted in meaning. Lewis and Barfield assert that this contraction of language occurs generally through passivity in human usage, while expansion of meaning occurs through human intention.

Evolving an Interior Language Leads to an Evolving Consciousness. In the past, humanity used an external and a material language to refer to the outer world of "nature." Over time the language became inner and immaterial by describing what took place inside individuals as humanity evolved an inner life. It is only to the extent that we use language to express a thing that we can really be said to be properly conscious of the thing at all. This is how we come to know ourselves. This fact is comparable to the experience we all went through as children, when our learning to speak corresponded to the way we began to identify objects in our environment. These experiences exist side by side as correlatives to one another.

This gradual historical development of an inner or immaterial language out of an outer or material one enabled us to become aware of an inner world in contrast to the outer one. The existence of ourselves as conscious individual beings is a reflection of the ability to abstract. This process occurs through the instrumentality of language and its changes over time.

We have paid a price for language's evolution into ever-more abstract forms. We don't have to continue paying the price, however. Our challenge is to retain indigenous perceptive capacities in a conscious way for the full benefit of the linguistic evolution we have been charting above.

The Poetic Role Today. I spoke about metaphor as a bridge to discover meaning and how metaphors become everyday language over time; as such, you can understand how language is a "forgotten and therefore used-up poet."[23] Human consciousness evolves because of these expanded meanings in language. When we encounter the poetic, we become conscious of meaning latent within the fluid reality inside the rigid lexical definition of words. Poets (and scientists) help us "see" this fluid nature of our language.

Totalitarianism and Language. Barfield occasionally expressed concerns regarding the potential for our world to move toward totalitarian states which would attempt to control language. This control, he warned, would significantly limit the human spirit, and thus stifle the evolution of human consciousness.

---

23 Heidegger, *Poetry, Language, Thought*, p. 208.

[Those] who are driven by an impulse to reduce the specifically human to a mechanical or animal regularity will continue to be increasingly irritated by the nature of the mother
tongue and make it their point of attack.... [If] they succeed
in expunging from language all the substance of its past, in
which it is naturally so rich, and finally converting it into the
species of algebra that is best adapted to the uses of indoctrination and empirical science, a long and important step
forward will have been taken in the selfless cause of the liqui-
dation of the human spirit.[24]

We see such a move in China, which has moved to forbid the
use of non-Chinese words in media such as "email," "Google," and
the like. This type of governmental action occurs out of fear of the
power of language to incite dissatisfaction with the government.
The government fears the ability of those who speak out to bring
conscious awareness to their situation. Paulo Freire's *Pedagogy
of the Oppressed* served as a means to bring to consciousness the
lived experience of those in oppressed countries (primarily in South
America and Africa) in the 1970s. This "new" awareness resulted in
a number of liberation movements in our world. Freire was banished
from Brazil at the time, though he was later welcomed back as a
hero in 1989.

Summary

Language plays a most significant role in human evolution. In
our exploration, we have participated in a historical look at language and how it changes, and stated that it is through a study of
language that we see a history of the thoughts of humanity.

In the context of our theory of knowledge, consider what we
have covered thus far: an examination of human consciousness
evolving from a collective consciousness to an individual one; the
proliferation of "objects" which has allowed science and technology to flourish; and, the way language (and consequently, meaning)

---

24   Barfield, *Poetic Diction*, pp. 13–14.

expands and contracts. It has also been pointed out that history is a history of thought. It is the past reenacted in the mind of the historian and the readers of history. History has an inside and an outside—any time you use a word you are in a sense reenacting a small part of it—this is the semantic approach to history we have been undertaking. We are moving closer to the core of the New Enlightenment. In the next chapter we will arrive at the epicenter.

Chapter 6

THINKING, REASON, AND MATTER

*"I can guarantee that you'd have no chance at all of getting
an inhabitant of the tropical forests of New Guinea to accept
even a hundredth of the discoveries of science. The other person has to have some comparable mental framework. You'd
have to educate him in a particular way for many years.
Similarly, people who haven't opened their minds to it could
never be made to accept the results of contemplative research.
There, too, some education is necessary. The goal of the sciences of what is reproducible, the hard sciences, is actually
not to solve metaphysical problems, nor to give meaning to
life, but to describe the material world as exactly as possible.
To say that reality can be reduced simply to matter and that
consciousness is just a property of the nervous system is no
more than a definition of the context in which science operates. Contemplative life, too, has its own rules, and the deep
conviction that comes from practicing it has, on the mind,
as much impact as any experiment whatsoever that can be
carried out in the material world. Observation of the nature
of the mind, from a purely contemplative point of view, can
bring about a certainty just as complete as observing a body
falling under the effects of gravity."*
—MATTHIEU RICARD (*The Monk and the Philosopher*)

We have arrived at the place in the journey where we can
begin to incorporate the way the human mind works into
a workable theory of knowledge. On the journey thus far you have
learned of the evolution of human consciousness and some of the
roles played by your mind and by language. I introduced you to an

essential distinction for our journey with the concept of the "unrep-resented" subatomic particles that are the essence of all matter, and began introducing vocabulary to discuss the mind and the dynamic process of cognition.

This chapter opens with a look at mind–body connections in medicine. We then address the core difference between an Enlightenment and a New Enlightenment experience of reality which leads directly to a look at "Reason." After defining Reason we will add a handful of new terms to our working vocabulary to lay a foundation for a bridge from an Enlightenment mind-set to a New Enlightenment one. Following the lexical section, I proceed on the journey toward the center of the book's argument. During the journey I ask for your patience. I will conclude with drawing some conclusions concerning the nature of the human experience of reality.

Mind–body Connections

January 31 to February 2, 2011, marked one of the strongest storms in the recorded history of the United States. The bliz-zard stranded hundreds of motorists on Chicago's Lakeshore Drive, effectively ended most commerce in Oklahoma for three days, disrupted outdoor activities for Super Bowl week in Dallas and brought two feet of snow across more than 1,500 miles from Oklahoma to New England. At the height of the storm I was in an airplane traveling from Florida to Minnesota. As the plane passed through considerable turbulence I smiled and enjoyed the "ride." Twenty years earlier I experienced just such a bumpy ride on a plane from Tokyo to Manila. At that time I did not smile. In fact, I experienced significant fear, bodily sweat, and a rejection of the contents of my stomach.

What changed? For one thing, my mind changed. Fear and uncertainty played a significant role in the distress my body experi-enced in the earlier trip. Experience and a calm self-talk resulted in a much different experience on the later trip. Perhaps there is more to the mind–body connection than the West would like to admit.

We have difficulty effectively articulating a mind–body connection. And when we do articulate a connection we start with the body and its material components. We seem to be unable to view the two as interpenetrated and working in a way that can be discussed and distinguished but not separated.

Another example I find to demonstrate our difficulty in talking about the mind and its relation to the body concerns the fact that in the United States psychologists are not allowed to "touch" patients. Yet, other "body workers," such as massage therapists, myo-facial release practitioners, and others, are allowed to do so. The implied reason is that psychologists cannot be trusted with the physical since they are dealing with the mysterious mind and could somehow be manipulative for some selfish benefit. Some psychologists avoid this difficulty by having one office for "talking" and another one across the hall for other methods that involve touch. It is as if science gets the body, psychologists get the mind and no one gets the holistic person.

Medicine. One researcher who has been working to overcome this strong disconnect between the mind and the body is Andrew Weil, M.D. He is an author of more than a dozen books and has conducted extensive research over thirty years on the role of the human mind in affecting health within the physical body. He appeared on the cover of *Time* in 1997 and 2005. *Time* also named him one of the twenty-five most influential Americans in 1997 and one of the hundred most influential people in the world in 2005.

In his many writings he notes that, in the current materialist paradigm of modern medical science, it is assumed that for a change to occur in the physical realm the cause must be physical. For example, it is well known that physical changes and imbalances in the autonomic nervous system cause physical problems such as high blood pressure, gastrointestinal issues, and circulatory disorders. Conventional medical treatments for these types of problems involve medicinal suppression (some of which are toxic) of the autonomic nervous system.

However, there are now almost four decades of mind–body connection research that show many of these imbalances have been caused by stress. Stress, you may know, is not physical but mental, and can be alleviated by increasing activity in the parasympathetic nervous system. Many mind exercises, such as biofeedback, progressive relaxation, medical hypnosis, and guided imagery, have been shown to increase parasympathetic nervous system activity and cause relaxation and bodily changes. The mind and the endocrine system are linked via neurochemical conversations that involve a constant back and forth. Thus, to relieve certain physical ailments you must lessen your stress—which can be done using only your mind.

Having previously been married to a family practice physician for a number of years, I learned anecdotally of many physicians who understand the mind–body connection and recognize that medicine is not the only way to treat physical issues. Family practitioners learn to take into account family history, current situation in life, and other contextual factors not normally viewed as essential to diagnosis and treatment of a physical malady. Insight gained from this approach has been aptly named "narrative wisdom." These physicians incorporate their knowledge of mind–body wisdom (even if they do not explain it in those terms) and offer words of encouragement or a re-framing of a situation to activate the parasympathetic nervous system.

As another example of the mind's influence on the body, Weil frequently comments on the respect and power most patients give to the words of physicians. Positive or negative words from a physician can have profound effects on physical responses of patients.

On a related issue, many people today could derive considerable benefit to their own well-being if they understood the power of their own thoughts, beliefs, and emotions and their effects on their physical health and overall wellbeing. Former National Institute of Health chief researcher and author Candace Pert speaks of health from the perspective of what one thinks, how one moves, and what one eats. She reports that more than eighty percent of most people's inner thoughts are negative. She also establishes a biomedical basis for emotion, explaining how our feelings, emotions, and bodies are connected through our mind.[1] The logical conclusion from these studies is that life can be dramatically altered based on one's own thoughts.

Mind–body medicine provides a fitting example for illustrating the central difference of approach and perspective of the two theories of knowledge we have been discussing in this book. The Enlightenment view takes what has already occurred—a sickness or physical difficulty of some sort—and tries to "fix" it with a physical solution. The New Enlightenment view looks for an holistic solution, not only to the current physical issue but also as a preventative to future problems, by altering one's mindset and behavior.

The Living Heart or Ignorant Knowledge

As we move closer to the core of the New Enlightenment, I want to briefly summarize the difference between the two avenues to knowledge from a perspective provided by Barfield. He predicted a period of years where there will be a battle for the Western mind between, on the one hand, this New Enlightenment theory of knowledge, and on the other hand, the Enlightenment and Postmodern theories.[2] From his perspective, it is because the Enlightenment ignored the role of the mind in producing the macroscopic world that a positive future is in doubt. He described the situation as a widening gulf between those for whom "knowledge means ignorant but effective power, and those for whom the individual imagination is the medium of all knowledge from perception upward."[3]

He compares the two different approaches to that of a very large automobile, with the automobile being a metaphor for the universe (this metaphor was briefly mentioned in chapter 1). Two types of

---

1   Pert, *Molecules of Emotion.*

2   Barfield saw postmodernism, with its materialistic base, as a natural outgrowth and an extension of an Enlightenment mindset despite their sometimes-conflicting emphases.

3   Barfield, *Poetic Diction*, p. 12.

passengers ride in the car, those who are interested in invisibles such as internal combustion, and the others who believe the means to discover how the vehicle works is to pull levels by trial and error. Eventually those of the second group conclude that ideas such as internal combustion are an illusion. They then conclude that their means of pushing and pulling levers is not simply a means to knowledge, it is knowledge. Barfield describes this type of knowledge as dashboard knowledge, with its ability to push, pull, and turn, but no awareness of what is under the hood.

This one-sided view of human experience, common to both modernism (Enlightenment thinking) and postmodernism, poses the greatest challenge to our world. The one-sided view focuses on the outside of matter and fails to look at the inside. This failure results in alienation from nature, despite the reality that we are in direct causal relation to nature. The New Enlightenment focus, as we have seen, begins with the interiority. The battle Barfield described will occur (or is beginning to occur) because of the entrenched power and moneyed positions of those with an Enlightenment mentality. Universities and foundations have established university chairs and grants that must use Enlightenment methods. Entire disciplines have built huge infrastructures of power and money all based on an Enlightenment worldview. Changing this will not occur easily or quickly.

But, in the end, the two approaches do not have to battle one another. Rather, the New Enlightenment, as it comes to prominence and is more broadly understood, will infuse the old paradigm of attention to the "outsides" with life and spirit, providing impetus for a new approach to science and to societal problems.

Not Passive Recipients but Active Thinkers. Recall that Enlightenment science and postmodernism take the view that our minds are passive recipients of sense data. Objects are believed to be a given. They "exist" without the human person. Any thought put into understanding the object must start with the assumption that the object itself is the starting point.

The New Enlightenment theory of knowledge does not follow this view. Rather than viewing the physical object as the starting point, it views the object as resulting from the process of thought as thought interacts with the unrepresented. Through the medium of language, active thought "creates" the object itself out of the unrepresented and does so through new ways of seeing. The lens for new ways of seeing come from organizing ideas and word concepts.

The Organizing Idea

In roughly 1609, Galileo "discovered" the mountains and valleys of the moon. What Galileo actually saw were not mountains and valleys but "a larger number of "spots" than could be seen with the naked eye. These were small and numerous, compared with the much larger ones with which everyone who gazed at a full moon was already familiar. Others could "see" these spots as well. But what did they mean? Galileo had not "seen" mountains. Only through an organizing idea that came to his mind did it occur to him that what produced this type of visual data was, in fact, mountains and valleys on the moon. The "discovery" was not what he had seen but the organizing idea that is of the mental world.[4]

To describe how organizing ideas work, remember that you filter all that you encounter through your senses. As you filter, you experience meaning. For example, if you see a yellow light at an intersection, you associate meaning with the light, its color, and its placement in your environment. Henri Bortoft describes the split second, unconscious process of receiving sensory data and converting it to meaning as the "organizing idea." These "ideas" organize sensory input.

The organizing idea is not on a plane or in a realm above the physical (such as is the case with Plato's Forms) but interpenetrated with it. Organizing ideas are "presencing it" or "there's-ing

---

4   Bortoft, *The Wholeness of Nature*, pp. 138–140.

it," the "it" being the object (a yellow light) we experience. What we "see" is meaning.[5]

Organizing ideas are not what is seen; they are the how of seeing. They are not like a mental picture of an object that you have in your mind when you see the yellow light. This is because, once you have a mental picture of an object, you have already traveled in your mind to a place that is temporally after the creative moment of the organizing idea. The organizing idea is the act of seeing what is there; it is the direct apprehension of what is there.

An organizing idea such as "table" is constitutive; it is the possibility of tables. This is in contrast to the typically abstract way we think of the term "table." Ordinarily, we think of that term as the composite term we create to identify a commonality found in certain similar objects. These objects are believed to be already "there" as a given. However, if you did not have the organizing idea "table," you would only experience unknown sensory data. Organizing ideas are how you see.

There are many of these organizing ideas that are the essence of a given society's figuration. This is why there is more than one way to see reality. There is much more to see than what we Enlightenment thinkers currently "see." Part of the active use of Imagination is to discover these additional ways to see our world and ourselves. In a parallel way we learn from linguistic theorist Hans Gadamer's philosophical hermeneutics that multiple interpretations can be true to a written text or an artwork and still maintain the integrity of the piece itself. The work is wholly there in each interpretation, no interpretation is the whole work, and the work maintains its unity in multiplicity.[6]

Forgetfulness of the how of seeing is the origin of "The Belief." None of the explanations of science as it is currently taught takes into account the active role of the organizing idea, despite the fact that modern quantum science asserts that one cannot investigate objects independently of the investigating subject (scientists).

---

5   Bortoft, *The Wholeness of Nature.*
6   Gadamer, *Truth and Method.*

"Reason," Thinking, and Trust

Two correlative developments form the essence of what I have described as the evolution of human consciousness throughout human history: 1) a strengthened ego for human individuals, previously discussed in chapters 4 and 2) the emergence of rational thought or reason, our focus in this chapter.

Dualists who hold to a strict separation of mind and matter, and materialists who do not acknowledge the existence of the immaterial, believe that the human capacity for reason evolved as humans evolved. That is, as biological life evolved from irrational nature, reason evolved as a by-product of biological evolution.

But does this make sense? This does not begin to answer how reasoning and the analytical thinking common to the Enlightenment developed. How can rational thought emerge from irrational nature? If you indeed submit that irrational nature produced rational thought, on what basis do you trust what this irrational nature has produced? How do you know that rational thought can be trusted? How do you even know of what rational thought consists?

Do you trust because, "Well, 'most' people trust rational thought so it must be right." If you simply go along because "most" people believe something, then we would still have slavery in much of the world and the caste system in India. Do you mean that you are going to trust what most people think "now" as opposed to 500 years ago? But how can you trust what scientists say is the nature of our world? How can you trust or know anything for sure? You may answer that what a person said was reasonable, that it makes sense. Then why do you believe what scientists are telling us about quantum physics? Surely that doesn't "make sense?" What is the basis of your view that something is reasonable?

Do you trust what postmodernists tell you, that the only meaning you can depend on is what works for you? "And," they follow, "if your meaning works for someone else and you can make a go of it, then have at it. Create whatever kind of social order you want to. None is better than another because there is no meaning, no truth, nothing trustworthy." Do you choose to follow this postmodern view that eliminates all meaning and knowing?

What I find interesting about the perspective of both modernists and postmodernists is that they assume they can convince you of their position if you take the time to listen. They believe in some form that they are "right" in what they assert. But, on what basis are they saying they are "right"? By doing so, they are appealing to something above and beyond material nature. They are appealing to some aspect of something we can call "reason."

If you believe that either postmodernism or modernism or the New Enlightenment is "true" in some sense, whether absolutely or partially true, then you are showing yourself to be a supernaturalist.[7] "Super" means above, higher in degree and quality, than nature.[8] By assuming that something exists other than irrational nature—that communication is meaningful and can be reasonable—true, false, understandable, muddy, and whatever other ways you can describe it—then you believe in something above the world of matter (nature). You show that you believe in "Reason."[9] In fact, I would assert, you participate in Reason every time you think or speak a valid thought.[10]

By the way, many agnostics and atheists, who would claim to be materialists and deny the validity of anything that does not have a material basis, behave as if they are supernaturalists as well. By this I mean that they appeal to Reason every time they present an argument to you. By being involved in reasoned discourse they participate in a realm that is not made up of matter. To understand Reason better, you can refamiliarize yourself with the New Enlightenment lexicon.

---

7   Barfield, *Worlds Apart*, p. 41.

8   In Latin *super* has the derivative *superare*, or to overcome.

9   I capitalize *Reason* to recognize that it comes before nature, is above nature, and is something that deserves the extra attention our language gives to word capitalization.

10 Much of the argument presented in the section on Reason comes from Barfield's brilliant dialogue in *Worlds Apart*.

A Lexical Pause

Collective representations—the forms of matter that commonly
appear when humans of a particular era participate with the
unrepresented; non-Enlightenment societies experience different representations than post-Enlightenment societies

Conscious participation—the awareness of being able to see in
both an Enlightenment and a non-Enlightenment way, resulting in different opinions and decisions about the problems of
society

Core morality—the realm of spiritual energies that present
themselves within the mind of those individuals who are
attentive to them

Evolution of consciousness—the development through human
history of the way humans are aware of the nature of
existence

Figuration—representing the sum total of a society's collective
representations

Imagination—the conscious and willful application of one's
mental ability to bridge from viewing to experiencing the
phenomenal world in a holistic way while maintaining a
subject/object perspective

Intuition—the way in which we can know something without
the need for analysis or rational thought

Mind—the human capacity for thought that is both particular
(in an individual person) and universal (means for thought
and knowledge are universal). The human brain serves as
a "mirror" for the thoughts of an individual's mind. When
a person is thinking, the person is in the universal world of
thought, though they are accessing it within the awareness of
their own individuality

New Enlightenment—a way of experiencing the world of objects
from the "inside," from the perspective of how the human
mind co-creates objects from the unrepresented

Organizing idea—the active potential that creates a scientific
insight—for example, a game of baseball is more than the
sum total of each activity that makes up the game (running,
throwing, hitting); it is an organizing idea without which

the activities that occur would be less meaningful. A bunch of people running around hitting and throwing balls with no organization is quite a different thing from an organized game of baseball with its official, or locally agreed-upon, rules.

Participation—the process where humans, with their sensory organs and their minds, encounter the unrepresented and experience the unrepresented as a form of matter

Percept—any single sense datum a person experiences

Primary imagination—the unconscious organization of the natural world possessed by virtually all humans

Reason—(n.) the preexistent and above-nature thought logic through which we can know truth from error as it relates to the objects of our world

Spirit—what is not matter, which includes, for example, the idea of courage, feelings, memories, rules, morals, organizing ideas, Reason. Synonym: *Being*

Unrepresented—the subatomic particles/waves as they exist prior to human *participation* (interaction); proto-matter, pre-matter, or potential matter

Word-Concept—the active potential that unites with a *percept,* resulting in the creation of the object associated with the language term

Understanding Reason

The word "reason" is based on the Latin *ratio*. This can be a numerical ratio such as three over four. Or, a ratio can be taken qualitatively—as in, A is related to B, as C is related to D. Using abstract ratio, or Reason, you can start from some fact and come to a conclusion. Individuals who believe arguments are worthwhile believe in the validity of rational thought. They demonstrate this by engaging in discussions and arguments where they can be convinced through logic of a particular point of view.

Here is an example to help illustrate. A man who believes there is a woman hiding behind a curtain may be either a) rational, because we know he saw someone go back there a while ago and hasn't seen her leave, or b) irrational, because he suffers from paranoia. If you assume that there is such a thing as truth and error at all and believe the man because of the reason he gives, then you assume that some part of the thinking process—his Reasoning—can be trusted and is not a product of irrational causes. Again, in practice this shows you to be a supernaturalist.

Reason, as well as thinking, is superindividual. It belongs to all and exists whether the man in the example above chooses to appropriate it or not. Reason is already "there" before you or I were ever old enough to know it. It existed prior to all human consciousness. Reason was there when the first human evolved consciously enough to be aware of it. When you appropriate Reason, you become consciously aware of something that already existed. We make sense of nature and of ourselves as individuals through the use of Reason.

Reason is the power of our thinking that takes the unity of our world, "divides" or abstracts it, and then allows for a reconnection to the unity. It brings consciousness—that is, awareness of the particular out of the unified. Self-consciousness, then, is awareness of ourselves as individuals abstracted out of the same unity.

We intuit Reason: We "know" Reason from within. We do not *perceive* Reason, since it does not come to us through our senses.

Using Reason to Understand "Spirit" and Matter. Reason is part of the world of "spirit." Think of "spirit" as anything that is immaterial. Examples of spirit include courage, a thought, an intention, or a mental picture. It should be mentioned again that critics might argue that courage, a thought, an intuition, and the like, are simply material brain states. I've already discussed the logical problems with this type of perspective in chapter 2. To summarize that discussion: intuition, thought, and courage all have corresponding material brain states, but the brain states are not the immaterial "thing" itself.

Perhaps the most obvious example of spirit is our awareness of ourselves as individuals. Spirit is what we are as persons, as individuals. I may recognize the physical matter of a person as their body, but what I really recognize is the "spirit" that is the being of another "I." Spirit depends on matter, not for its existence, but for its expression. Relationships are between two individual spirits, not the phenomenon of the two physical bodies.

Word-Concepts: The Substance of Reality

"Word-concepts" are the fundamental substance of thought. They are formed in an individual when that person combines thinking with perception. Anything that enters your awareness through your senses is, by definition, a percept, which has immediate conceptual information connected with it. We learn many of our word-concepts as children, though we continue to learn new ones all the time. These concepts allow us to "see" things we would not see without them.

To reiterate, a person who had all the organs of perception but had done no thinking in relation to percepts—such as a previously deaf or blind person—would perceive only a "blooming buzzing confusion" and could not comprehend it. Words allow a person to identify objects. We never consciously experience such a blooming confusion of a world unless we have the experience of those who had never heard or seen and were suddenly able to do so. Other than that, all of us combine percepts and concepts and even systems of concepts before we even know they have been cognized. As far as most of our conscious experiences are concerned, the world comes at us already organized, unless one can slow down one's mind through meditation to see these organizing ideas.

The Billiard Ball. The percept's connection with its concept is recognized *after* the act of perception (very quickly after!), but their belonging together is determined by the situation itself. To illustrate this, Barfield uses an example of one billiard ball striking a second billiard ball. Were we not to think, we would only perceive the movement of energy of some sort but would lack a way to organize that percept. We would have no sense that one ball hitting another would have some predictable effect. It requires thinking to have the concepts of a ball and its motion. These concepts—sphere, movement, impact, velocity, flat plane, gravity, friction—are all concepts that have to be learned. And they are concepts that are, given the most common context, "true" for everyone.

From the time we first understand that a moving ball on a flat table will move in a straight line (assuming no side-spin on the ball and enough velocity) and that another stationary ball, on the first ball's line, will collide, we know it as something that we can predict will happen the next time we are in the same situation. Therefore, when we see the next ball rolling toward the other ball, we quickly and automatically make a connection with the concept in our head and know that the one ball will hit the other.

When you or I perceive something with one of our senses, or when we feel something inside of us, it is part of our private world. However, as soon as we think, we allow concepts to unite with perception or feeling. At the point of thinking we are no longer separate but part of the world of rational thought. In essence, thinking is happening in us and through us.

Through thinking we are given the element that unites our particular individuality with all other individuals. When you think a concept, such as our previous example of the colliding billiard balls, you are thinking a concept that is true for all people who have the same concept. *This is why you are able to communicate, discuss, argue, and make progress in understanding with others—because you share the world of thought and the thought logic of Reason.*

A percept—experiencing an object that enters our field of awareness—is one side of the coin; the word concept—provided by our mind (but belonging to the universal world of mind)—is the other side of the coin. The link between you, the subjective individual, and the movement of the one ball in space, the objective, is not built by any real process or perceptible event but is actually built by Reason through the word-concept we have learned.

Mind Preceding Matter

The previous discussion of Reason, word-concepts, and percepts leads to some conclusions about the nature of our existence.

- Given that the appearances and phenomena of our world are made manifest (visible and capable of being experienced) through human interaction with the unrepresented, I conclude that they (the appearances and phenomena of our world) are *spirit manifested as matter.* Spirit is the field of potential from which matter emerges and forms into what we experience as materiality. Spirit—the immaterial—depends on matter, not for its being, but for its expression. Matter is literally spirit "pressed out"—"ex" "pressed," expressed, in physical form.
- Should you wish to look for the source of spirit, understand that spirit is not a "thing." You will not find out what "thing" produced spirit since a "thing" cannot be of the same substance as the phenomena. "Things" are produced out of the world of spirit, not the converse.

There is no evidence whatever for the assumption that parts (or particles) preceded the wholes and that the world was actually built by putting together the units into which our minds divide it, as a house is built by stacking bricks. It is foolish to take a house to pieces to find out that it is made of bricks, and having done so, to say that the bricks built the house.[11]

As Samuel Taylor Coleridge points out:

In the world, we see everywhere evidences of a unity, which the component parts are so far from explaining, that they necessarily presuppose it as the cause and condition of their existing as those parts; or even of their existing at all.... Analyze the seed with the finest tools, and let the solar microscope come in aid of your senses, what do you find? Means and instruments, a wondrous fairy tale of nature, magazines of food, stores of various

---

11   Barfield, *History, Guilt, and Habit*, p. 13.

sorts, pipes, spiracles, defenses—a house of many chambers, and the owner and inhabitant invisible![12]

Clarifications. Spirit, therefore, is not that which is perceived as matter but that which *is*. It is what we are as beings. The same relation between matter and spirit exists in each individual. The perceiver is the "being." Any relation we have with another person is between the two individual spirits, not the phenomena of the two bodies. The bodies are the "expression" of the individual beings.

I do not mean to say that matter is an illusion as would be the point of view of much of Buddhist and other Eastern religion and philosophy. But insofar as we're concerned, matter exists; it is just not merely objectified material. Matter is an interpenetration of our minds with the subatomic material of the universe.

Matter and Its Relations to Language. The unrepresented are like a wave or field prior to interacting with our senses. What we experience as the familiar world are our "collective representations." As soon as you or I come in contact with the unrepresented, we perceive a world of forms, shapes, and "things." These "things," which include size, color, shape and other qualities, appear to us this way because of the unconscious activity of thinking as it interacts with the unrepresented. The only connection we have, as outside observers, with these unrepresented phenomena is at the point of thinking.

The relation between our collective representations and language is of the most intimate nature. We name that which we have identified and abstracted out of the unrepresented field. Anyone who insists that words and things are in two mutually exclusive categories of reality has confused the phenomena with the unrepresented. The collectively represented, since we have abstracted them and they are part of our consciousness, are the physical side of our consciousness. Our consciousness provides the "insides" to the physical, such as a wooden table. The history of this consciousness is a history of a *given period's* figuration. The phenomena undergo change in

---

12 Coleridge, quoted in Barfield, *What Coleridge Thought*, p. 44.

response to the evolution of consciousness itself. This means that our participation with the unrepresented evolves as well, which changes our very perception of the world.

Individual Consciousness. Another point of clarification is that, while spirit precedes matter, this is not *individualized* spirit or *self*-consciousness. It is the one consciousness, a unity of consciousness, out of which individuality evolved through a historical process described previously (see chapter 3). Individuals today evolved from non-individuated humans to individuated beings, which is the current status of our genus.

As I mentioned, Charles Darwin's *Origin of Species* was written at a period of history when self-consciousness had so fully achieved prominence in our understanding that individuals could no longer feel any participatory link with material phenomena. Consequently, it is understandable that Darwin did not conceive of a concept of a prehistory where matter and mind were interpenetrated. He assumed matter preceded mind since it preceded *self*-consciousness. This is a logical outgrowth of the Enlightenment theory of knowledge by which Darwin operated.

In the New Enlightenment theory we began with our human mind and how it functions. This led us logically to recognize that the world of Reason operates within the world of thought. When we enter the world of thought, Reason is already there, operating prior in time to our awareness of it. This also led us to understand Reason as prior to the production of the material world we experience. Within this universal world of thought we experience our individual consciousness. However, early *Homo sapiens* experienced a different type of consciousness, one that did not have individuality in the way we currently experience it in our Enlightenment figuration. I referred to this earlier as world consciousness. Human self-consciousness evolved through a compression or focusing modality tied directly to the evolution of language into its current highly abstract form. This evolution of *Homo sapiens* is reenacted in each and every child born within our Enlightenment mindset world. In a wonderful image, children have "to wrestle subjectivity out of the world of experience by polarizing that world gradually into a duality."[13] Humanity as a species has accomplished the same through its history.

Though it is beyond my purposes in this book to give an explanation, I believe that the same type of compression or focusing modality produced the world of matter as we experience it. I believe the logic is sound when one begins not with an object "out there" but starts within the mind and sees how the world is created from within. The science for demonstrating this is in its nascent form in the scientific writings of German literary genius and naturalist Johann Goethe.[14] There are some in our world today who are beginning to seriously study the ideas behind his theory. I expect that as understanding of the New Enlightenment spreads, many more of our world's bright minds will begin integrating this science with our current materialistically based science.

Ramifications. The New Enlightenment theory of spirit-first presents a number of issues that deserve to be addressed. I will discuss two of the most direct.

Chance or Intention. To theorize that matter condenses from spirit rather than exists independently requires a discussion of the driving force behind this condensation and evolution. From where does this drive originate? Is the drive a form of intentionality?

Remember, our behavioral interpretation of nature is not, as has been generally assumed, a reflection of fact but an arbitrary mental construct. When you assume that the Darwinian theory of evolution reflects the whole truth, you have bought into the view that we live in a material universe governed by chance. This is the view, as

---

13 Hocks, "The Other Postmodern Theorist: Owen Barfield's Concept of the Evolution of Consciousness" (*Tradition & Discovery: The Polanyi Society Periodical XVIII*, 1991–92), p. 32.

14 Bortoft, *The Wholeness of Nature.*

I have asserted, that brings about so much of our Western world's alienation to ourselves and to nature.

It's incredible that modern science's two most cherished material theories, evolution and quantum theory, are based on an axiom of randomness. If rational thinking tells us anything, "Chance" is not a valid hypothesis for any focus of research. Yet this is what we are told. How can *chance* be the basis of *order*—that is, the hierarchical order of life on earth with its sequential development and the highly symmetric and regular structure and behavior of matter? The concept of chance is precisely what a hypothesis is supposed to save us from. But neither Darwin nor the quantum theorists of today can avoid concluding that chance, or mathematical probabilities, determine the underpinnings of life today.

But if not chance or probability, what other options do we have? The other end of the continuum from chance is intention. When we present intention as an option, we naturally move toward the realm of theology. Are there divine beings or a divine Being that works invisibly behind the evolution of human consciousness? You must answer "yes" if you understand mind and Reason and its role in creating our awareness of our individuality and our awareness of the material world in which we currently live. I will not attempt to address the nature of this Being or beings here. However, this affirmative answer allows us to replace Darwin's chance-ridden natural selection with intentionality, which is (in my opinion) a more satisfying conclusion. Intentionality does not eliminate the overall tremendous insights of the study of biological evolution. It adds to it and will alter it in ways that are, as of yet, to be completely understood.

Our Relationship with Nature. Another ramification of a spirit-first theory illuminates our relationship with nature. Because our consciousness is the inside of the material nature that we experience on the outside, our relationship with nature is sacramental and, consequently, worthy of reverence and respect. When we recognize this relationship, we have reason to avoid viewing the manipulation of nature as simply a means to an end. This can have a direct effect on how we make decisions concerning our means of living on this earth. Given that nature is part of us and we are part of it, and were we to inherit her, we can no longer simply view her as an instrument from whom we should take advantage. While Francis Bacon is often incorrectly viewed as responsible for the phrase "nature must be put on the rack and her secrets tortured out of her," the sentiment of doing this has been central to the Enlightenment's view of nature. We continue at the risk of destroying nature.

Definition of Life and a Way to Proceed Forward

This new theory of knowledge concludes that we live in a spirit-first world. It goes beyond the materialistic theory that concluded that an irrational nature produced Reason. This leads us to consider the question of life; what it is and how we can reinterpret our definition of life. The question is a huge one and its implications range from how we define life in micro-biological terms and whether or not any artificial machines, such as robots, can ever be "alive." If we conclude that being "alive" means having some sort of feelings or consciousness, then we can rightfully ask whether or not something like a stone is alive. If our answer is "no," then what about the atoms of the stone with their swirling subatomic particles? Are they alive? If not, how are they always moving?

Modern Biology's Identity Confusion. Modern biologists display classic signs of identity confusion. On the one hand, they seem obsessed with mechanics. Steve Talbott, a senior researcher at The Nature Institute commenting on this tendency, writes that "no cellular entity or process receives an exemption; everything has been or will be baptized a 'mechanism.'" He notes a vast biological literature lexicon including genetic mechanisms, oncogenic mechanisms, DNA repair mechanism, and on and on. Each and every article contains the use of these types of phrases in virtually every section.

In contrast, biologists also use a decidedly different language when they speak about the processes of living organisms. In this way, their language closely represents the language of the New Enlightenment.

In article after article their studies of living cells are filled with such words as "inherit," "issue an integrated response to current conditions," "make limited predictions about future environmental changes," and "insight into the thought processes of the cell." Nobel Prize winner Barbara McClintock even went so far as to declare: "In the future we should try to determine the extent of knowledge the cell has of itself, and how it utilizes this knowledge in a 'thoughtful' manner when challenged." Biologists do not use these terms when they described the cells within a corpse of a living organism.

Talbott traces their dilemma to their need to divide the whole into parts in an attempt to understand the whole by understanding the parts. Their fundamental reductionist approach, taught to them in their science classes, prevents them from seeing more completely what they discover in the living cells they study. What remains is a kind of confusion. They see these living processes in cells. But they do not know how to talk about this as it relates to the whole organism. They struggle to define "life" or "living." Talbott continues:

> Beginning with a molecular-level analysis of the simplest, single-celled organism extant today and proceeding through all the ever more complex creaturely orders, we see no sudden discontinuity in the play of meaning and inwardness—a play that progressively comes to a focus in the individuated centers of consciousness we know as our selves.[15]

What Talbott shows through biological studies themselves is that biologists see life as an inwardness with its predictions and responses and thought processes and knowledge. They simply have a hard time coming right out and saying so. In contrast to the confusion of modern biology, C. S. Lewis in his *Studies in Words* reports that most

---

15   Talbott, "The Language of Organisms," in *Being Human* 2011 (Ann Arbor, MI: Anthroposophical Society in America), pp. 36–37); online: http://www.anthroposophy.org/fileadmin/nfm/bh-1/being-human-2011-01-Language-of-Organisms.pdf.

philosophers who have written about the definition of life believe "life" to be a given; a sort of factual, preexistent unity. This is quite similar to the descriptions described above concerning Reason and thinking, since they are means of describing a preexistent unity.

Physicist David Bohm adds to the general common sense view of "life" as a preexistent unity with a discussion of how one can begin to investigate life as it manifests itself in nature. You will note that he does not, in this passage, postulate intentionality or causality in nature but only what could be termed first principles of life in nature.

> In nature nothing remains constant. Everything is in a perpetual state of transformation, motion and change. However, we discover that nothing simply surges up out of nothing without having antecedents that existed before. Likewise, nothing ever disappears without a trace, in the sense that it gives rise to absolutely nothing existing at later times. This general characteristic of the world can be expressed in terms of a principle which summarizes an enormous domain of different kinds of experience and which has never yet been contradicted in any observation or experiment, scientific or otherwise; namely, everything comes from other things and gives rise to other things.
>
> This principle is not yet a statement of the existence of causality in nature. Indeed, it is even more fundamental than is causality, for it is at the foundation for the possibility of our understanding nature in a rational way.[16]

As Bohm states, the essence of the natural life is that it is productive in the wide sense of evolving phenomena from other phenomena. There are important differences with his perspective and that of Enlightenment science.

First, Bohm begins with the observation that nature perpetually moves, evolves, and transforms. This is in direct contrast to a focus on static entities, which was the starting point of Enlightenment science. Bohm's starting point does not involve the goal of discovering the tiny particles that serve as building blocks of nature. He does

---

16   Bohm, *Causality and Chance in Modern Physics*, p. 1.

not set as a goal to be able to reduce the world to its quantitative dimensions. His fundamentals are movement and energy, change and interdependence. It follows from this that even in stones, atoms are always moving, interacting, transforming. Stones in this sense are alive.

Second, he observes that every "thing" comes from other "things" which give rise to yet more "things." Evolution and change are always taking place; life at its core is energetic and transformative. These starting points result in very different answers to questions of life from those common to Enlightenment thinking.

In order to understand the constantly transforming, energetic nature of natural life and the role our minds play in interpenetrating with the unrepresented to produce natural life, we need a way to think that differs from the way we think while under the control of "The Belief."

The means to help us is Imagination, and as we move through the next chapter we will examine how Imagination allows us to bridge this gap between the world of spirit and material world.

Summary

Over the past two chapters, I have looked at language and its role in bringing our awareness to ourselves and to nature. First, I looked at the positive of abstract thinking: 1) it helps us make sense of the vast amount of potential sensory data available to us, 2) it produces subjectivity and, consequently, individuality of persons, and 3) it allows for the advancement of technology. I also examined the other side of abstraction and how easily one can believe that the objects of our material world are all that exists, resulting is enslaving ourselves to the lifeless images of one's own abstractions and feeling lonely in the universe.

We then looked at Reason and saw how it allows us as individuals to participate in its world of thought. We have been tempted to revere objects as ends in themselves and to idolize the understanding. Yes, we experience the culmination of our detachment through abstract understanding, but we awaken to our true nature that we share with others through the connection we have to the world around us and to one another. With this awakening we have the potential for a different and higher order of attachment within the unity that is found in the interpenetration of mind and spirit.

We delved also into the "thinking" that is within each of us as individuals and which we share with all. One of Barfield's favorite quotations on these topics from Rudolf Steiner provides a fitting summation of the role of thinking:

> Thinking must never be regarded as a merely subjective activity. Thinking transcends the distinction of subject and object. It produces these two concepts just as it produces all others. When, therefore, I, as thinking subject, refer a concept to an object, we must not regard this reference as something purely subjective. It is not the subject, but thought, which makes the reference. The subject does not think because it is a subject, rather it conceives itself to be a subject because it can think. The activity of consciousness, in so far as it thinks, is thus not merely subjective. Rather it is neither subjective nor objective; it transcends both these concepts. I ought never to say that I, as individual subject, think, but rather that I, as subject, exist myself by the grace of thought.[17]

Using logic, I declared that mind precedes matter. I continued by pointing out that the definition of life common to most people has congruence with the theory of the New Enlightenment. We concluded with a look at some of the fundamental elements of new science. In the next chapter we move our attention from this foundational theory of knowledge to the active role we each can take in our lives and in the world and how this is accomplished through the use of Imagination.

---

17 Barfield, *Poetic Diction*, pp. 208–209.

Chapter 7

IMAGINATION

"How often people speak of art and science as though they were two entirely different things, with no interconnection. An artist is emotional, they think, and uses only his intuition; he sees all at once and has no need of reason. A scientist is cold, they think, and uses only his reason; he argues carefully step by step, and needs no imagination. That is all wrong. The true artist is quite rational as well as imaginative and knows what he is doing; if he does not, his art suffers. The true scientist is quite imaginative as well as rational, and sometimes leaps to solutions where reason can follow only slowly; if he does not, his science suffers."
— Isaac Asimov *(The Roving Mind)*

"What is originality? To see something that is as yet without a name, that is as yet impossible to designate, even though it stares us in the face. The way it usually is with people, it is a thing's name that makes it perceptible to them in the first place.—For the most part, the original ones have also been the name-givers."
— Friedrich Nieztsche *(Sämtliche Werke)*

Isaac Asimov provides us with an excellent encapsulation of one of my main themes. Moving society forward requires both imagination and science. In this chapter I will provide a more specific meaning for the word imagination and use it in capital form—Imagination—because of what I believe is the importance of the term. A summary of where we've been and where we're headed in this chapter can be seen in the following simple chart:

Spirit: what is not matter

Imagination: the bridge between matter and spirit
Reconnecting to spirit, the living unity
Accessing core morality

Primary tools of the Imagination
Feelings
Intuitions
Will
Intellect

Imagination lies inherent in each person. We use one form of it at all times. Barfield calls this form "primary" imagination and, by this term, he refers to the fact that we are always taking the vast amount of sensory data coming into our physical body and converting it into a figuration of objects. This, as we have seen, occurs unconsciously. This will not be discussed further.

Secondary imagination, or Imagination, is the type that Asimov describes above and is indirectly similar to what we think of when we say "use your imagination." Its primary focus concerns seeing connections, seeing wholes, rather than seeing parts or objects. The moment of an Imaginative insight is one where "seeing" and "understanding" are one and the same. It is the moment when a gestalt comes into focus.

This latent Imagination, in contrast to the more free-flowing, undisciplined type we often employ in a more fantasy-like manner, involves a disciplined, rigorous use. As such it can be developed and enhanced. Given that I am suggesting we can learn to not only use Imagination but to trust it, it is important to discuss the topic of trusting something that is subjective; by subjective I mean that it is something we do inside ourselves as individuals.

Trusting the "Subjective"

Discussing trust as it relates to the subjective may at first glance seem odd, given we have learned from quantum science that we cannot fully trust in objective science, as there is no such thing. Ironically, the realm within our minds is known today as the "subjective," even though it is our mind that creates the "objective" word. I believe we can and should put our trust in Reason, which is "subjective" in this way. In order to trust Reason, however, we must understand the role our minds serve in interacting with the world. As our insight into our own mind becomes clearer, we learn to "know" immediately what should be trusted.

An example will make it clear how we "know" we can trust Reason. Consider Amy, who is looking for a job. At a party she is introduced to Jarrod, a friend of Amy's friend. Jarrod manages a local call center. After talking with Jarrod about her own job search, he tells her that he may have a position for her and that she should apply for it as soon as possible. The following Monday morning Amy phones human resources at the call center and mentions the encounter with Jarrod.

What can you say about her "memory" of the encounter? Can it be trusted? It is after all "subjective." How does Amy know that this is a memory and not either a fantasy of her mind's creation or an internal psychological mishmash which developed because of an episode of a television sitcom she watched? The memory of meeting Jarrod presents itself in her mind as a memory. She *knows* she had the encounter. It is an event that presents itself immediately in her awareness. She *knows* it can be trusted.

Malcolm Gladwell's **Blink.** Another example of trusting the subjective comes from Malcolm Gladwell's number-one international bestseller, *Blink: The Power of Thinking without Thinking*. In the introduction to the book Gladwell asserts that "the most important task of this book is to convince you that our snap judgments and first impressions can be educated and controlled."[1] He proceeds to attempt to demonstrate that you can learn enough about how your mind works so that you can rely upon and have confidence in your

---

1   Gladwell, *Blink*, p. 13.

instincts and intuitions. The implicit power underlying Gladwell's assertion, the power providing confidence, is the power of Reason.

Reason and its tool, logic, underlie most of the solutions to the crime and legal novels and films that many of us find so compelling. As we follow a story line, we draw conclusions, not only about the logic of the outcome, but also by applying Reason to evaluate the motivations and intentions of the characters. Any time we find the conclusion of a story satisfying, we have applied Reason to determine that the conclusion is both tenable and moral (more about the "moral" in the pages ahead).

As we prepare to dig more deeply into Imagination, let's look at one of the exciting frontier applications of it—that is, the reconnection to spirit in the world of big business and government.

Otto Scharmer and Theory U

Theory U, an approach to group strategy and planning, is built on the theory of the New Enlightenment. Otto Scharmer, protégé of world-renowned business theorist Peter Senge, developed Theory U (the "U" suggests the visual pattern of his methodological flow), which theorizes that the way in which we attend to a situation determines how the situation unfolds: *"I attend this way, therefore it emerges that way."* His chief method, termed "Presencing," seeks to activate a "generative listening" on the part of leaders so that they might attend to a source of ideas generated from the universal realm of mind. This type of listening he describes as an "holistic perspective that also includes the more subtle mental and intentional spiritual sources of social reality creation." As a practical social technology, Theory U offers a set of principles and practices for collectively creating the future that, in his words, "wants to emerge."[2]

Whether at a retreat for the leadership of Fujitsu, at a regional education summit in Frankfurt Germany, at an MIT think tank, or for companies as diverse as GlaxoSmithKline, Hewlett-Packard, Federal Express, or PricewaterhouseCoopers, Scharmer guides

---

2 Scharmer, *Theory U*, p. 13.

leaders in Presencing, a multi-step practice of focused attention followed by complete openness, in order to foster access to the Source of intuition of new ideas. He explains:

> Across all levels, systems, and sectors we face basically the same problem: the challenges we face require us to become aware and change the inner place from which we operate. As a consequence, we need to learn to attend to both dimensions simultaneously: what we say, see, and do (our visible realm) and the inner place from which we operate (our invisible realm, in which our sources of attention and intention reside and from which they operate).... I [have] found that there are four different places or positions that each gives rise to a different quality or field structure of attention. They are: 1) I-in-me: what I perceive based on my habitual ways of seeing and thinking; 2) I-in-it: what I perceive with my senses and mind wide open; 3) I-in-you: what I tune in to and sense from within with my heart wide open; and 4) I-in-now: what I understand from the source or the bottom of my being, that is, from attending with my open will. The four field structures differ in the place from which attention (and intention) originates: habits, open mind, open heart, and open will, respectively. Every action by a person, a leader, a group, an organization, or a community can be enacted in these four different ways.[3]

In his text on Theory U, Scharmer describes the process he recommends for strategic leadership to address significant problems. At first his approach seems common to strategic planning: "Create the intention to solve a problem, dive into it, work like crazy, break the flow (stop), pay attention to the ideas that start to slip in through the back door of your mind; then develop and embody that idea."[4] However, the way an organization "break(s) the flow" and "pay(s) attention to the ideas that start to slip in"—part of Theory U's "generative listening"—differs from most strategic sessions in that he seeks to create an environment where new ways of viewing

3   Ibid., pp. 10–11.
4   Ibid., p. 423.

and responding to a situation can emerge; in essence, the future emerging in the present.

He describes an example of how OXFAM Great Britain (OGB) realized why existing approaches to the HIV pandemic of southern Africa were inappropriate and ineffective. They were able to "presence" an organizing idea that allowed them to "see" the problem differently. The organizing idea concerned the fact that the issues faced by southern Africa are systemic and interconnected with world affairs. Treating the problem as one merely requiring better education, or access to condoms, at the local level would never address the underlying problems of large numbers of the work force living far from areas of employment, requiring months of living away from home. Effectively addressing the pandemic can only be done through a large system-wide approach with large-scale changes.

The Organizing Idea and Theory U. Organizing ideas are what meet us in moments of inspiration or insight. This is what the people at OXFAM discovered when going through Scharmer's Theory U to address the AIDS epidemic. The organizing idea of the larger systemic issues of employment and living conditions rose to meet them, bringing clarity for how they saw the environment. The organizing idea "presences" the new way to see.[5] This organizing idea emerged from the realm of spirit in a way that Scharmer refers to as originating in the future. The emergence of the new way to see led OXFAM to a completely different strategy to meet the challenge of the now-seen environment.

Scharmer speaks a language that differs from the familiar time-worn mechanistic and deterministic language. He speaks the language that allows for insights to come from the insides. He speaks the language of the New Enlightenment and the use of Imagination:

> So far the primary focus of our modern sciences has been, by and large, limited.... But now we need to broaden our view of

---

5   The term *presences* is borrowed from Bortoft, p. 137.

science to include the other capacities to grasp the truth, including applied technologies (*techne*), practical wisdom (*phronesis*), theoretical wisdom (*sophia*), and the capacity to intuit the sources of awareness and intention (*nous*).[6]

Imagination and Its Use

Imagination serves as our bridge between matter and spirit. It is conscious and active. It is that which sparks the creative power of a handful of the leading poets, scientists, and artists. This is the creativity described in chapter 5 as what uses metaphor as it creates and expands meaning. Certain artists, poets, and scientists, such as Einstein, are, in many ways, conscious of what they are creating (though perhaps not at the exact moment of creation but in their immediate reflection post creation). Organizing ideas come and are communicated via metaphor, which is the recovery of meaning after abstraction has occurred (e.g., Newton and the word *gravity*).

Another common example of Imagination may help. When I look at my children, I don't see their physical bodies as much as I see whole people with histories, feelings, thoughts, wishes, questions, and desires. In this way Imagination is a relation between spirit and matter that at once maintains and transcends the contrast between the two. Consider your experience of texting your children or playing an online game such as "Words with Friends." Your Imagination carries your experience of the relationship you have with them, such as from the humor they convey to the "inside" references you share together.

Compare that to how we often categorize people for certain purposes—for example, into two genders, or into those who are tall, short, blue-eyed, brown-eyed, and so on. Clearly we get value from that. But we would never "reduce" the individual to some sort of sum of their physical characteristics. It requires Imagination to "know" a person in the fullness of who they are, both inside and outside.

---

6   Scharmer, *Theory U*, p. 16.

While Imagination transcends the distinction between spirit and matter, mere perception—perception without Imagination—separates. It is the sword thrust between spirit and matter. It is this type of perspective that allowed Descartes to partition all being into the mutually exclusive categories of extended substance (the physical) and thinking substance (the thought world). Mere perception, however, is not what we normally do when we look at or listen to another being. We use Imagination to heal this Cartesian thrust that cleaves spirit from matter.

It is possible to look at nature in the same way we look at individuals—as both an expression of spirit and as a collection of physical objects. Understanding living plants, animals, and humans requires a "both/and" perspective. We can learn to see holistically and objectively. Although Johann Goethe has pioneered methods for doing so, Westerners must develop the capacity to participate in his process, which takes time and practice.[7] One cannot truly study nature in its fullness from a Cartesian perspective. The science of the future will spend as much time understanding the "insides" as it has spent learning of the "outsides," and in the process of doing so will allow our post-Enlightenment world to reconnect to the living unity within which our life as human individuals connects, while also placing us in direct contact with the source of all human morality.

Reconnecting to the Living Unity. As individuals and societies move toward reconnecting with life's source in spirit, much can be learned from non-Enlightenment people. This can be accomplished in two ways: first by learning from the writings of the past, and second by interacting more effectively with current peoples who remain in a non-Enlightenment mindset. Through the use of Imagination we may be able to connect to the organizing idea that allows us to "see" the way others see and, hence, gain needed knowledge to address societal needs.

---

7   An excellent place to start is Bortoft, *The Wholeness of Nature.*

Learning from the Past. People who lived in the past lived with an interconnection to the living unity, but they did so without individual consciousness. We cannot forget this. I mentioned earlier that modern scholars often read the writings of non-Enlightenment literature and assume the writers were consciously applying modern thought when they describe their experience of the world. Because modern scholars interpret their writings in a post-Enlightenment way, they conclude that these writers used metaphor in their descriptions. This could not be further from the truth. These non-Enlightenment writers provided what can be termed "primary meanings," but they were not given consciously, nor were they metaphors; they were lived. These "primary meanings" constituted a communication from within their own consciousness of their directly lived experience. They were therefore not "creative" in the way we understand meaning-makers of today, the scientists and "poets" who bring new or rediscovered meaning into our purview. Writings from a non-Enlightenment writer can better be compared to that of a researcher, reporting their lived experience. Poets and meaning-makers of post-Enlightenment time attempt to retrieve the unity that pre-logical humanity apprehended as a matter of course.

Learning from Indigenous Cultures: Zimbabwe. Indigenous knowledge is the knowledge resident in people who are born and raised in an indigenous cultural context. Ways of knowing, thinking, and creating in such a culture are commonly passed down from generation to generation without reference to textual methods. Individuals learn by seeing, doing, and mentoring by local masters. Such knowledge is constructed, in context, through multifaceted interactions and conversations.

In Zimbabwe, and many other nations with indigenous societies, countless generations have been perpetuated through this process of knowledge re-creation. The problem with this type of generational pass-down is that if the mentoring/learning process is interrupted or changed, prior knowledge can be quickly lost. Since the colonization of Zimbabwe in the nineteenth century, many new technologies, foods, and ways of knowing have been introduced to the people. Western education, schooling, and literacy have advanced knowledge based on non-indigenous values, needs, and ways. As a result, the last two generations of villagers have been isolated from the old indigenous ways.

For many, this may seem to be a valuable sign of progress. More recently, however, evidence of the negative consequences of these changes surfaced. This was particularly evident in the drought and resulting famine of 2004 to 2005. Prior to colonization, villagers did not fall into famine when regular and varied droughts hit their region. Many elders in the Gutu district of Masvingo province in southern Zimbabwe routinely lived past a hundred years of age. This was at least partially because the villagers used indigenous knowledge of "traditional" methods to prepare and preserve sufficient food reserves. But when Western farming methods were adopted, the region was unable to maintain enough reserves to bring them through the drought and resultant famine of the past few years. Many more died due to lack of available food than have died in past times of similar drought and famine.[8]

Since 2004 and 2005, the elders of the region revived the indigenous knowledge of crop cultivation, storage, and cooking. A number of younger villages have learned to grow the traditional millets and store food reserves for decades at a time. Many Zimbabweans believe that these elderly people hold more kinds of indigenous knowledge in areas such as animal husbandry, medicinal herbs, and land stewardship, to say nothing of the pride of culture that can lift and infuse the quality of life of the community—all knowledge that is valuable for the future well-being of Zimbabwean peoples.

Means for effective communication with those from a non-Enlightenment mindset and means for preserving captured knowledge can be challenging. My purpose is not to detail how this can be effectively done (though it will include granting larger amounts of indigenous autonomy and offering outlets for cultural preservation

---

8   Interview with Chidara Paul Muchineripi, Chinyika (Zimbabwe), community leader and Steve Kada, business consultant, Zimbabwe, Feb. 11, 2010.

and language translation), but to note that we have much to gain from a reconnection with these societies, as they have still unforeseen means of helping us connect with Spirit and procuring methods that our world needs today.

Freewill. Our imaginative reconnection to the living unity of Spirit will be conscious. We have free will to make choices as to where our awareness will be focused. We are able to do so because we are autonomous individuals and free will is part of what being an individual entails. When we take the time to use our Imagination in connecting with spirit, we will encounter our free will and its correlative, morality. Every choice has a moral element.

Connecting to Core Morality

When I discussed the mockingbird in chapter 4, I briefly examined how thinking takes place and the role of one's habits, memory, imagination, will, and feelings. Patient observation of your own thinking allows you to become familiar with the interplay of these mental constructs. As you gain skill in this type of observation, you can discern the various motives that lead you, for example, to follow a chain of thought or, for another example, to attempt to justify some of your own behavior. In doing this type of observation you will connect with a core morality. In time you will realize that this core morality is central to your individual decisions, your exercise of free will. Similarly, core morality is crucial to decisions made at the highest levels of government and commerce. Many leaders do not acknowledge the morality that is at the center of public policies.

One of the byproducts for those who practice the work of Otto Scharmer's Theory U Presencing involves the time and space given to connect at the deepest level to this moral core. The four levels of listening mentioned above (I-in-me, I-in-it, I-in-you, I-in-now) are designed for just the possibility of morality to surface. Numerous reports from practitioners illustrate the intensity and power of sessions that reach a deeper level of communication and understanding.[9]

9   See the Presencing Institute Community at community.presencing.com.

Only when time is taken to penetrate the inside can one discern the forces of morality. This holds true for individuals and collectives such as corporations and governments. For a means to help you examine your own connection to a core morality and to examine these thoughts further, I refer you to the writings of Arthur Zajonc.[10]

Societal Issues, Equality, and the Moral Center. With few exceptions, the history of the governments of large-scale societies involves the significant use of power and control, often to the detriment of large numbers of people. It seems that the dark side of human morality emerges when individuals or groups of individuals exercise direct control over others. Greed, envy, and pride lead to atrocities as horrific as genocide. Individuals who perpetrate these evils hide behind some ideology as if the ideology can mask their own individual depravity. Modern Western governments have attempted to offset this human tendency with the way they are constructed. The United States' three branches of government attempt to provide a system of checks and balances for the benefit of the citizens of the country, and for the most part this has worked remarkably well domestically.

As it relates to international affairs, the challenges are more complex given the different histories, cultures, and beliefs of nation-states. We have yet to evolve a means to handle the dark side of human morality as a more globalized world. Organizations such as the United Nations have helped in some limited ways.

The current universal demand for individual rights is a recent phenomena historically, a result directly attributable to the evolution of consciousness. This leads to the many complex issues challenging our world today. Politics (as well as history) is a science, in the proper sense of the word, because it depends ultimately on method—that is, on illuminating how the mind participates in Reason. There remains a great deal to do in order to bring a world filled more with peace than with suffering and war. Not until nations can sit at a table and acknowledge their interdependence, their connection to

10   Particularly, Zajonc, *Meditation as Contemplative Inquiry.*

spirit, and their common morality can the darker aspects of human nature be effectively addressed.

With the proliferation of easy communication and the advancement of Western education, people the world over cry out for equality. Equality is rooted in the strength of the super-personal idea of justice, which draws from our moral center. However, there is a distinction between equality, particularly in the rule of law where it is essential for protecting individual rights, and uniformity, which requires that everyone be the same. Individuals are not all the same—we are not uniform. Some easily confuse equality with uniformity; the latter is often a direct result of personal envy. We are all interdependent, but we are not all uniform; we are merely equal relative to justice.

The significant issues in our world require reasoned deliberation from a place of generative listening in order to access the moral center of the source of life. This is best done by having a theory of knowledge that acknowledges this moral center. In the next chapter I speak about ways that the abilities of Imagination can be developed. These abilities allow for improved deliberations and negotiations between competing interests. However, I want to close this chapter's look into the use of Imagination by mentioning two current issues. These issues are important because they impact the economic fabric of our world and help explain the profound increases in alienation and depression in post-Enlightenment societies.

Financial Crises. Our world's current financial crises stem from profound moral, ethical, and spiritual failures. Many signs point to the fact that our neo-liberal economies are predicated on an annual growth of three to five percent per year. More than enough analyses and critiques have shown the impossibility of sustaining that type of growth. For our world to move toward sustainable economies, change must take place on the inside. The issues are moral, ethical, and spiritual, but as a society we have no theory of knowledge on which to base a public discussion. In the public sphere we do not know how to talk about the moral principles that inform us and can help us see more clearly. We also do not adequately know how to speak about the economic principles that will allow for us to pursue life, liberty, and happiness. These must be balanced and brought out in the open. It does little good to express criticism without finding a solution. I believe some are in the offing and could be profoundly beneficial for our world to consider;[11] however, change has to be first on the inside.

Free Markets and Multinationals. Multi-national corporations and free market forces often work counter to moral principles that would work for the betterment of our world as a whole. Hyper vigilance concerning the value of stock leads corporations to choose approaches that enhance self-interest often at the expense of world needs and the environment. Monsanto and Cargill's investments in genetically modified organisms (GMOs) has the ostensible purpose of improving world food supplies. However, concern over long-term environmental impact of GMOs and the corresponding green revolution with its emphasis on chemicals and pesticides gets pushed to the side in favor of the more immediate increased quantity of foods and subsequent increased stock values. One can imagine an approach that takes all the issues and finds a clearer moral center than the one that is current for these corporations, influenced as they are by the interests of their stock holders. Some argue that free market forces will balance out these imbalances in perspective. I disagree in this faith in free markets. I would rather take responsibility and stewardship of the environment and of society, and seek for solutions that arise out of a holistic moral core. I should caution that I am not recommending that any work with GMOs is inherently wrong. There may be quite useful value in pursuing GMO research. My concern is the inherent motivation of some of the multi-nationals and the seeming hyper-confidence in a free market system to work for the good of humanity and the earth.

---

11   See three works in particular: Médaille, *The Vocation of Business;* Lessem and Schieffer, *Integral Economics;* and, Rima, *Spiritual Capital.*

Mental Illness and Moral Imagination. In order to perceive another's spiritual activity in speech, gesture, countenance, and body language we must exercise moral imagination. Moral imagination can be defined as the ability to discern various possibilities for acting in a given situation and to envision potential help and harm that are likely to result from a given action. All of us can recall a time when we implicitly trusted someone; a stranger, a lover. For so many in the Western world, the ability to exercise moral imagination has been lost. Many of those live with some form of mental illness

Endemic to the increase in mental illness and depression, Barfield tells us, is the sense that life on earth has little to no meaning. Consequently, individuals either distract themselves with material pursuits or find a haven in a traditional religion where they can live out their days waiting for the reward at the end of the journey. Barfield diagnoses the main cause of the alienation many feel toward life as a result of living in an Enlightenment mindset. He uses the case of schizophrenia to demonstrate what occurs when this alienation is experienced in its fullness:

> But what the self of each of us feels isolated from, cut off from, by its encapsulation in the nakedly physical reality presented to it by the common sense of contemporary culture, is precisely its own existential source. The trouble is, that such an empirical self, founded as it were on its own physical encapsulation, is a false self, without reality.... The true Self of everyone remains united—not co-extensive but united—with its original source in the spirit. And the mental illness now recognized as schizophrenia comes from the frantic efforts, sometimes aggressive, sometimes defensive, made by the imprisoned personality to fortify and preserve this fictitious self—which is really a nothingness—from destruction. Instead—and that way sanity lies—of taking the hint, as it were, and learning to abandon it in favor of the true Self...the patient's unstable behavior is thus a disguised form of evasive action. He is determined, as R. D. Laing has put it, "to evade becoming himself."[12]

---

12 Barfield, *History, Guilt, and Habit*, pp. 52–53.

Barfield exhorts us to recognize not our individuality—that is a given—but our common origin in spirit, or as he terms it, "Self." This recognition, he asserts, allows for individuals to find meaning in life. Without such a connection, history is fundamentally meaningless and life consists merely of "one damn thing after another," resulting in depression, illness, withdrawal, or indulgence.

Summary

I hope you have been convinced in your reading that you have an inside, and that it is within yourself as an individual that you will find the path to the knowledge of the New Enlightenment. Those who are aware of the evolution of consciousness resulting in individual freedom will be primed to grasp our spiritual inheritance. When this inheritance is grasped, we can make its substance available to the many societal ills, bringing authentic wisdom to much needed arenas. Where existentialists bore the heavy burden of societal ills without hope for the future, New Enlightenment thinkers will be able to take on the responsibility for societal ills with new confidence born of the knowledge of the source of our existence in spirit.

We connect with spirit, not for escape, but for the source of what will make human life successful in the succeeding millennia. In many ways, it is as if Western humanity is moving from being a teenager to that of an adult. To do so requires embracing what we find inside, learning how to access the sources of the insides, and effectively living. These sentiments are expressed beautifully by Alfred Lord Tennyson:

> I trust I have not wasted breath:
> I think we are not wholly brain,
> Magnetic mockeries; not in vain,
> Like Paul with beasts, I fought with Death;
>
> Not only cunning casts in clay:
> Let Science prove we are, and then
> What matters Science unto men,

At least to me? I would not stay.

Let him, the wiser man who springs
Hereafter, up from childhood shape
His action like the greater ape,
But I was born to other things.[13]

Overcoming the alienation brought on by an Enlightenment mindset requires Imagination. Imagination will allow us as individuals and as societies to reconnect to the source of our existence. We can begin by learning from non-Enlightenment peoples. As we apply Reason and Imagination to examine how our minds work, we will come directly in contact with the forces and energies through which our thoughts are generated. We can then begin to identify the moral forces at work within us. These thoughts provide a fitting conclusion in preparation for the next chapter's presentation of the laws, means, and roles of a qualitative science, along with an examination of the abilities of Imagination.

Moving on

Enlightenment	⟶	New Enlightenment
Scientific method	⟶	Knowledge of qualities
Language abstraction	⟶	Synthesis of Mind and matter

---

13 Tennyson, "In Memoriam A.H.H.," cxx; online at http://www.online -literature.com/tennyson/718/.

Chapter 8

KNOWLEDGE OF QUALITIES

*"As to knowledge of nature and knowledge of God, if knowl-
edge is the doing of a jigsaw puzzle with atomic events, there is
no more to be said. But if it is really a participation through the
symbol in the symbolized, it is a different matter. It is a different matter if the sequence of a divergent followed by a convergent evolution is a positive fact and not just a cleverly invented
analogy; if humanity was originally one and indistinguishable
in the unconscious and is now aiming to become both one and
many in full consciousness...then our knowledge of nature is
very relevant...for it is only by ceasing to regard nature as a
specter that we can hope to inherit her as a kingdom.*

—OWEN BARFIELD[1]

*"Knowledge is our destiny. Self-knowledge, at last bringing
together the experience of the arts and the explanations of
science, waits ahead of us."*

—JACOB BRONOSKI[2]

We arrive now at the culmination of this journey into the
world of the New Enlightenment. Whether you were previously aware of it or not, your reading of popular writers such
as C. S. Lewis, J. R. R. Tolkien, Deepak Chopra, Marianne Wil-
liamson, Wayne Dyer, and Candace Pert, whose flourishing writing
grounds itself in most of the principles of the New Enlightenment's
theory of knowledge, introduced, though perhaps in a hidden way,

---

1   Barfield, *Worlds Apart.* p. 271.
2   Bronowski, *The Ascent of Man*, p. 437.

this knowledge to you. Also, many of you engage in activities that root in the very same soil—activities such as Waldorf education, the Transition Town movement, permaculture development, and the work of The Nature Institute. My hope is that, having read about this type of thinking, you are now beginning to experience more consciously the fertile source that grounds these activities.

Spirit Source	Descent into matter		World consciousness		Dawn of individual consciousness	
Pre-history		2700	1000	500	0	1000	1500

Spirit Source Descent into matter   World consciousness   Dawn of individual consciousness

Pre-history   2700 1000 500   0   1000   1500

   Diversity of species   Beginnings of psycho-social convergence

   Unconscious knowledge of nature   Language abstraction begins and grows

                                              Self-awareness, developing ego

With a simple timeline flow we see an evolution of the development of individuality and its many societal ramifications, such as democracy. As our world converges and we, in essence, become less diverse, it is incumbent upon us to have a new way to think. No longer can we remain in our abstractions. We must find ways to reconnect to the source of all life. As we move into our future, we can and must shape this reconnection.

In this chapter, as a way to wrap up this volume's journey, I will provide an outline of an expanded science by presenting a beginning sketch of the fundamentals, abilities, and roles of which the new science of the reconnection of mind and matter consists. Following that I will present a few methods and resources that enable individuals and groups to access the sources of the internal dimensions of this science. You will remember that knowledge of the interior starts with qualities (the way your mind interacts with the unrepresented), since, as we have learned, that is how the world presents itself to us. As such it mandates an exploration in understanding and practice of the interpenetration of the interior of our minds with the outsides of objects. No longer can we afford to ignore this science. Otherwise, our technology will destroy us, either due to human ignorance of the moral consequences of our actions or through a complete loss of meaning in life.

Fundamentals to the Theory of Knowing the Qualities

As much as Enlightenment science has been guided by basic laws of matter, knowledge of qualities requires as a minimum an understanding of the following fundamentals:

1. The objective "outness" of physical phenomena occurs and is known through the awareness of human subjectivity. We provide the "insides."

2. Western societies must learn, practice, and pass on knowledge of how the mind works in conjunction with Reason. This leads directly to the study and practice of the power of the will and the intentions that come with its use.

3. Reason shows the unity we as a species share with one another and with all of nature.

4. Spirit (Being) comes prior to existence (existing as a conscious individual). We become conscious of Being only by means of existence. Having become conscious of our existence we understand through Reason that Being must be prior. This is comparable to the fact that, without seeing, we would not know that we had eyes; but having seen, we know that eyes must be anterior to the act of seeing.

5. The science needed for our future requires combining today's science with the knowledge that comes from studying human history and the evolution of consciousness. Science will continue to involve research using vigorous methods and verification as it engages a disciplined Imagination.

6. The construction of new models for social innovation requires understanding the self and the moral forces that influence our selves. There is a sense in which the individual in a state (governmental entity) exists for the state, only when it is also acknowledged that the state is in each individual. Or rather, when we shall have not merely acknowledged it, but embodied the idea in a constitution, perhaps the most compelling example of which occurs in the Constitution of the United States.

Abilities of Imagination

All humans have some ability to use the muscles of their bodies, whether for gross motor movements such as running or fine motor movements such as buttoning shirts. Some have more natural ability than others. But, with training, most humans can improve their abilities. Likewise, all humans have the ability to use Imagination. Some are naturally gifted; think Albert Einstein and Ralph Waldo Emerson. Most of us have latent abilities. For those with latent abilities, having been raised under the "The Belief," we may need quite a bit of training to learn how to use and to improve upon what we have. As of yet, Western education systems (with the exception of the Waldorf approach) do not discuss these abilities regularly nor do they provide systematic training as to how to work with them. With an understanding of the New Enlightenment this should change. The following list is not meant to be exhaustive.

1. **Feeling.** To learn effectively about how your will works with your thinking, you must learn how to observe and then use your feelings as a means to perception; you must use your feelings as precision instruments for investigating quality. Feeling is the field where the tension between the two poles of conscious and unconscious operates. There is a concept of objective feeling that can be used as a means to clearer thinking and deeper perception. Any competent poet or artist knows that.

Goethe described a method of investigation into the nature of plants by using his own sense of feeling.[3] Through his method he introduced to the world an understanding of plant metamorphosis. He described this use of feeling much like the experience one has when paying attention to the major and minor keys of music. With plants, he notes experiencing the alternate expansion and contraction, which characterizes the growth-process itself.[4]

---

3   Another good starting place for information on Goethe's scientific work can be found at www.natureinstitute.org.

4   Goethe, *The Metamorphosis of Plants.*

2. **Contemplation and observation.** Again I refer you to the scientific methods pioneered by Goethe and practiced by many from Michael Faraday to Werner Heisenberg. Goethe viewed and studied nature as the expression of spirit. His painstaking observations of color resulted in a description of the qualities of how phenomena are perceived, not an analytical mathematical measurement. His understanding of how the human mind works and how it interacts with the qualitative phenomena we experience allowed him to conclude that Isaac Newton's error in his theory of color involved the trust of mathematical calculations over the sensations of the human eye. He points out that one can view color as waves or vibrations, but in doing so you lose color itself altogether.[5]

Ironically, "The Belief" promotes trust in the observations of the senses but does so by beginning with the outsides of the phenomena while failing to recognize their insides. Science, starting with the outside, seeks to break down objects into their constituent parts. Goethe's methods, starting with how the object is perceived within the observer, starts with form as it is observed. With plants, for example, you never see the completed plant in its full form. It is always in a flux, changing at every moment in time. It is always unfolding; the only way to envision its fullness is to understand it as a totality of ever-changing forms. There is a rhythm to the plant's unfolding and cyclical expansion and contraction. Think of the ultimate contraction of the plant in the seed. The plant goes through phases of leaf growth, flowering with the organs of fertilization, the growth of its fruit, with a return to the seed, which "dies" but is passed on to the next generation during the next cycle of the plant's life, rebirth. During its "life" there is a seasonal choreography of daily leaf movements, sap circulation, opening and closing of the flower chalice, and the phases of transformation resulting in the seed. It has its own internal chronometer synched with the rhythms of the earth.

The insect kingdom is, of course, intimately related to the cycles of plant life and earthly rhythms. Light from the precise

---

5   Goethe, *Theory of Color.*

intersection of earth's position relative to the sun activates the adrenal hormones of insects in conjunction with the phases of fertilization necessary for the plants. Looking into ways to synchronize with potentially advantageous insect traits is a characteristic endemic to the New Enlightenment.

This focus on the essence of form results from a different perspective—from inside out rather than outside in. What science, by definition, omitted was even the potential for viewing any role for spirit. Scientists were to be objective and eliminated any "subjective" inside-out perspectives from their observations and experimentation. Of course, we have seen that this dichotomy was a chimera. Unfortunately, however, an entirely different way to look at the world has been relegated in large measure to an artifact of history, an approach to understanding our world that has "lost" in the "battle" for supremacy. Now science as we know it dominates the field. Overcoming the prejudice against Goethe's methods requires convincing huge institutions that another method is needed to join with the scientific method. We need what was left behind.

Fortunately, slowly but steadily, the number of researchers adopting Goethe's methods is growing, and the work of an influential international organization, The Nature Institute, founds its approach on his methods. Physicist Arthur Zajonc provides a description of the results of the practice of Goethean methods:

> Our true relationships in life are never to the material side of things. Reflect for a moment and you will recognize that you love your child or your garden or a poem because you have worked your way through its exteriority to an interior relationship with it. Of course the fragrance of lavender occurs via olfactory...but we sense through matter to the soul of the world...because we have gained fluency in an inner language of soul, we are well prepared for the challenging of a dawning new reality that defies materialistic

conception...perception and reflection become the systole and diastole of the mind.[6]

3. **Concentration and openness.** Concentration and openness are twin abilities that constitute the essence of the Presencing work of Otto Scharmer's Theory U summarized in the previous chapter. These abilities, when disciplined and consciously practiced, form a polarity of energy that results in intuition. Many of the world's faiths, particularly in the East, have much to teach the West in the development and practice of these disciplines. In the East these practices are often, although not always, associated with particular religious or spiritual traditions. Examples of these practices include meditation, yoga, prayer, contemplative arts, shamanic dancing, and contemplative movement.

The nature of modern technology designed to promote easy distraction does not help individuals learn about the power of concentration and openness, nor does this technology facilitate creativity or Imagination. Practice in concentration and openness helps counter technology's influence and, if applied regularly, cultivates social and emotional intelligence.

4. **Wonder and reverence.** In chapter 1, I mentioned that one of the results of "The Belief" involved the loss of awe. While a young child might express awe at the magic of light flooding a room, such a natural reaction often becomes stifled or shelved for adults who are "busy" with activities and responsibilities. Too often, this results in increased feelings of depression and alienation. Wonder and reverence are abilities of the soul. They can be deepened. Two quotations, one from Chogyam Trungpa and the other from Albert Einstein, say this very well:

> Appreciating sacredness begins very simply by taking an interest in all the details of your life. Interest is simply applying awareness to what goes on in your everyday life—an awareness

---

6   Zajonc, *Meditation as Contemplative Inquiry*, p. 120.

while you are cooking, awareness while you are driving, awareness while you are changing diapers, even awareness while you
are arguing. Such awareness can help to free you from speed,
chaos, neurosis, and resentment of all kinds.[7]

The most beautiful thing we can experience is the mysterious.
It is the source of all true art and all science. He to whom this
emotion is a stranger, who can no longer pause to wonder and
stand rapt in awe, is as good as dead: his eyes are closed.[8]

5. **Empathy.** Economist Sam Rima developed an inventory seeking to measure what he terms "spiritual capital." In his compelling
research into economic systems, he identified spiritual capital as a
missing ingredient in many governmental economic systems. Such
"capital" only results from going inside oneself and recognizing the
ontological interconnected nature of the world. When one has this
internal experience, one then develops a sense of personal responsibility toward others and becomes willing to undertake personal
action on behalf of the others.[9]

Governments and corporations often view its citizens as "things"
rather than as persons. When this happens, the organization has
lost its connection to Source. It may "succeed" for itself, but for the
world as a whole it will have failed to exercise its power in ways
that cultivate human dignity and meaning. That is a net loss for
our world.

An Interconnected Whole. These abilities of Imagination emerge
from within the soul. But they are not only for individuals. They
also work collectively when organizations or governments nurture,
develop, and practice them. To develop and use them requires time
and attention and, for those deeply entrenched in "The Belief," a
grounding in the theory of the New Enlightenment.

---

7   Chögyam Trungpa, as quoted, http://www.contemplativemind.org/about/faq
.html.

8   Einstein, *Living Philosophies.*

9   Rima, *Spiritual Capital.*

Four Roles for the Future

Under the theory of the New Enlightenment, we as a species have an opportunity to consciously evolve. In order to do so we must decide to do so. To accomplish this we will need four types of individuals:

1. Scientific innovators—these are rare individuals who shift human consciousness with their intuitive insights into the nature of phenomena. Examples include Francis Bacon, Isaac Newton, Galileo, Charles Darwin, Louis Pasteur, Albert Einstein, and David Bohm

2. Scientific clerks—these are the individuals who take existing ideas and technologies and refine and improve them by applying them in new ways. Examples range from those who straddle both categories, such as Thomas Edison and Al-Jazari, to most working scientists and engineers who research and investigate specific details of phenomena in order to follow up on the imaginative work of those in the previous category

3. Poetic creators—those such as William Shakespeare, Thomas Jefferson, Johann Goethe, Ralph Waldo Emerson, Leo Tolstoy, Mahatma Gandhi, Nelson Mandela, and Ibrahim Abouleish, who introduce new genres of literature and ways of designing social life by externalizing the wisdom and meaning they discern or intuit into words

4. Poetic clerks—those who both imitate and popularize the wisdom gained from the creators. This category of individuals includes those with design, marketing, communication, and political science expertise

Only through Reason and Imagination can we be sure anything exists outside of us. It is with these tools that the New Enlightenment proffers an innovation of reality. Our understanding of this reality points behind itself as both the source of and opposition to this understanding. Steeped in the stony landscape of logical contradiction, bound by its own horizon, "The Belief" is no more; the New Enlightenment is intact.

BIBLIOGRAPHY

Abouleish, Ibrahim. *Sekem: A Sustainable Community in the Egyptian Desert.* Edinburgh: Floris Books, 2005.

Ackerman, Diane. *Deep Play.* New York: Vintage Books, 1999.

Arnold, W., and M. Page (eds.). *The Nebraska Symposium on Motivation.* Lincoln: University of Nebraska Press, 1970.

Arntz, William, Betsy Chasse, and March Vicente. *What the Bleep Do We Know?: Discovering the Endless Possibilities for Altering Your Everyday Reality.* Deerfield Beach, FL: HCI, 2005.

Asimov, Isaac. *The Roving Mind.* Buffalo, NY: Prometheus Books, 1983.

Barfield, Owen. "The Case for Anthroposophy," in Rudolf Steiner, *Riddles of the Soul.* Great Barrington, MA: SteinerBooks, 2012.

———. *History, Guilt, and Habit.* Middletown, CT: Wesleyan University Press, 1979.

———. *History in English Words.* Great Barrington, MA: Lindisfarne Books, 1967.

———. *Poetic Diction: A Study in Meaning.* Middletown, CT: Wesleyan, 1973.

———. *The Rediscovery of Meaning and Other Essays.* Middletown, CT: Wesleyan University Press, 1977.

———. *Romanticism Comes of Age.* San Rafael, CA: The Barfield Press, 1966.

———. *Saving the Appearances: A Study in Idolatry.* Middletown, CT: Wesleyan University Press, 1988.

———. *Speaker's Meaning.* Oxford: Barfield Press, 2011.

———. *What Coleridge Thought.* San Rafael, CA: The Barfield Press, 1971.

———. *Worlds Apart: A Dialogue of the 1960s.* Oxford: Barfield Press, 2010.

Bellow, Saul. *Humboldt's Gift.* New York: Penguin, 2008.

Bohm, David. *Causality and Chance in Modern Physics.* London: Routledge & Kegan Paul, 1957.

———. *Unfolding Meaning: A Weekend of Dialogue with David Bohm.* London: Routledge, 1996.

Bortoft, Henri. *The Wholeness of Nature: Goethe's Way toward a Science of Conscious Participation in Nature.* Great Barrington, MA: Lindisfarne Books, 1996.

Bronowski, Jacob. *The Ascent of Man.* Boston: Little, Brown, 1977.

Camus, Albert. *The Stranger.* New York: Everyman's Library, 1993.

Cranstron, M. *John Locke: A Biography.* Oxford: Oxford University Press, 1985.

Derrida, Jacques. *Of Grammatology.* Baltimore, MD: Johns Hopkins University Press, 1976.

Eddington, Arthur. *The Nature of the Physical World.* Cambridge: Cambridge University Press, 2012.

Edwards, Clive A., et al. (eds.). *Sustainable Agricultural Systems.* Ankeny, IA: Soil and Water Conservation Society, 1990.

Einstein, Albert. *Living Philosophies.* New York: Simon & Schuster, 1931.

Emerson, Ralph Waldo. *Essays,* 2nd series. Charleston, SC: Nabu, 2010.

Feynman, Richard P. *The Pleasure of Finding Things Out: The Best Short Works of Richard P. Feynman.* Cambridge, MA: Perseus Books, 1999.

Frankl, Viktor E. *Man's Search for Meaning: An Introduction to Logotherapy.* New York: Pocket Books, 1963.

———. *The Unheard Cry for Meaning.* New York: Simon & Schuster, 1978.

Freire, Paolo. *Pedagogy of the Oppressed.* New York: Continuum, 1970.

Gadamer, Hans-Georg. *Truth and Method,* 2nd rev. ed. London: Sheed and Ward, 1989.

Gentner, Dedre, and Susan Goldin-Meadow (eds.). *Language in Mind: Advances in the Study of Language and Cognition.* Cambridge, MA: MIT Press, 2003.

Giddens, R. (ed.). *J. R. R. Tolkien, This Far Land.* London: Vision Press, 1990.

Gladwell, Malcolm. *Blink: The Power of Thinking without Thinking.* New York: Little, Brown, 2005.

Goethe, J. W. *The Metamorphosis of Plants.* Cambridge, MA: MIT Press, 2009.

———. *Theory of Color*. Mineola, NY: Dover, 2006.

Gregory, R. L. *Concepts and Mechanisms of Perception*. London: Duckworth, 1974.

Grene, Marjorie. *The Knower and the Known*. Los Angeles: University of California Press, 1974.

Heidegger, Martin. *On the Way to Language*. San Francisco: Harper, 1971.

———. *Poetry, Language, Thought*. New York: Harper and Row, 1975.

Heisenberg, Werner. *Physics and Philosophy: The Revolution in Modern Science*. New York: Prometheus, 1958.

Husserl, Edmund. *Introduction to Logic and Theory of Knowledge: Lectures 1906/07*. New York: Springer-Verlag, 2009.

Isaacson, W. *Einstein: His Life and Universe*. New York: Simon & Schuster, 2008.

James, William. *The Principles of Psychology*. Cambridge, MA: Harvard University Press, 1981

Jaynes, J. *The Origin of Consciousness in the Breakdown of the Bicameral Mind*. Boston: Houghton-Mifflin, 1972.

Jones, R. *Physics as Metaphor*. Minneapolis, MN: University of Minnesota Press, 1982.

Jung, C. G. *Synchronicity: An Acausal Connecting Principle*. Princeton, NJ: Bollingen, 1973.

Kuhn, T. *The Structure of Scientific Revolutions*, 3rd ed. Chicago: University of Chicago Press, 1996.

Lessem, Ronnie, and Alexander Schieffer. *Integral Economics: Unleashing the Economic Genius of Your Society*. London: Gower, 2010.

Lewis, C. S. *Studies in Words*. London: Cambridge University Press, 1960.

Linderman, Albert. *The Deaf Story: Themes of Culture and Coping*. Ann Arbor, MI: UMI Dissertation Services, 1997.

Médaille, John. *The Vocation of Business: Social Justice in the Marketplace*. New York: Continuum, 2007.

Mitchell, Peter, and Kevin Riggs (eds.). *Children's Reasoning and the Mind*. Hove, UK: Psychology Press, 2001.

Moyer, Richard, et al. *McGraw-Hill Science*. New York: McGraw-Hill, 2002.

Nadel, L. (ed.). *Encyclopedia of Cognitive Science*. London: MacMillan, 2003.

Nietzsche, Friedrich. *The Will to Power*. New York: Vintage, 1968.

———. *Sämtliche Briefe: Kritische Studienausgabe in 8 Bänden*. (G. Colli and M. Montinari (eds.). Berlin: de Gruytoer,1980.

Pert, Candace B. *Molecules of Emotion: The Science behind Mind–body Medicine*. New York: Simon and Schuster, 1999.

Postman, Neil. *Technopoly: The Surrender of Culture to Technology*. New York: Vintage Books, 1992.

Revel, Jean-François, and Matthieu Ricard. *The Monk and the Philosopher: A Father and Son Discuss the Meaning of Life*. New York: Schocken Books, 1998.

Rima, Samuel D. *Spiritual Capital: A Moral Core for Social and Economic Justice*. London: Gower, 2012.

Sacks, Oliver. *The Man Who Mistook His Wife for a Hat*. New York: Touchstone, 1998.

Scharmer, C. Otto. *Theory U: Leading from the Future as It Emerges*. Cambridge, MA: Society for Organizational Learning, 2007.

Searle, John R. *Consciousness and Language*. Cambridge: Cambridge University Press, 2002.

Sheldrake, Rupert. *Dogs that Know When Their Owners Are Coming Home*. New York: Three Rivers Press, 1999.

Steiner, Rudolf. *The Case for Anthroposophy*. Oxford: Barfield Press, 2010.

———. *Intuitive Thinking as a Spiritual Path: A Philosophy of Freedom*. Hudson, NY: Anthroposophic Press, 1995.

Watters, Ethan. *Crazy Like Us: The Globalization of the American Psyche*. New York: Simon & Schuster, 2010.

Weiss, Paul A. *The Science of Life: The Living System—A System for Living*. Mount Kisco, NY, Futura, 1973.

Zajonc, Arthur. *Catching the Light: The Entwined History of Light and Mind*. London: Oxford, 1995.

———. *Meditation as Contemplative Inquiry: When Knowing Becomes Love*. Great Barrington, MA: Lindisfarne Books, 2009.

INDEX

Abouleish, Ibrahim 66, 67, 160
abstraction 42, 97–99, 103, 133,
    141, 151, 153
  limits of 99
  process of 97
alienation 48, 115, 129, 147, 149,
    151, 158
Al-Jazari 160
alternative thinkers xiii, xvi
Aquinas, Thomas 71
Aristotle 46, 71, 103
Asimov, Isaac 135
astronomy 22
Athene 46
Auden, W. H. xix

Bacon, Francis xv, 50, 51, 130,
    160
Baldwin, James 52, 56
  his book *Notes of a Native Son*
    56
Bantu (languages) 38
Barfield, Owen vii, 40, 88, 152
  author's introduction to xix
  his book *History in English
    Words* 53, 104
Begley, Sharon 29
Belief, The xii, xiv, xix, xxii, 1,
    4–9, 12–14, 58, 62, 100,
    104, 106, 156, 158, 160
  resulting in mental illness 7–11
Bellow, Saul xx, 1
biodynamic
  astrology 70
biodynamic agriculture xxii, 66,
    67–69
blindness 33

"blooming buzzing confusion"
    123
body language 149
Bohm, David 132, 160
Born, Max 27
Boroditsky, Lera 88, 89
brain states 23, 28, 122
Bronoski, Jacob 152
Brothers Karamazov, The
    (Dostoevsky) 53

California Institute of
    Technology 37
Cartesian divide 50, 51, 142
causation 26, 31
Chichen Itza x, 79–81
Chopra, Deepak xiii, xviii, 152
Civil Air Patrol 4
Coleridge, Samuel Taylor 45, 125
collective representations 35, 37,
    64, 81, 120, 126
concepts 25, 29, 44, 93, 94, 101,
    105
  formation of 116, 123–125
conscience 49, 54
consciousness x, xiii, xvii, xxi,
    16, 28, 31, 34, 63, 68, 72,
    79, 81, 84, 96, 99, 101,
    103, 122, 126, 134, 160
  evolution of 39–61, 69, 82–83,
    85–90, 102, 106–108, 110,
    118, 120, 129, 147, 150,
    154
  group 8
  individual 127–128, 131, 143
convergence 38–39
Copernicus xvi

CPSIA information can be obtained
at www.ICGtesting.com
Printed in the USA
FSOW02n0227040716
22322FS